AEOLUS
Ruler
of
the Winds

Sailing adventures around
the Essex and Suffolk coast.

Shirley Baker

www.essex100.com

Published by Summersbook (UK) Ltd.
Rutland House
90 – 92 Baxter Avenue
Southend-on-Sea
Essex SS2 6HZ
www.essex100.com

AEOLUS Ruler of the Winds
First published June 2013
Written by Shirley Baker
© Copyright Shirley Baker
June 2013

Reprinted February 2015
Reprinted July 2016

British library cataloguing in Publication Data
A catalogue record for this book is available from
The British Library.

ISBN 9780955229589

Typeset by Hutchins Creative

Printed by 4edge Publishing
7a Eldon Way
Eldon Way Industrial Estate
Hockley Essex SS5 4AD

Sea Walk

The wild wind laughs – and I laugh too,
Clutching my coat which the wind blows thro';
My friends the sea-gulls scream in glee –
'I love the wind and the wind loves me!'
I stand by a wall, my hand to my hat
Watching the wind, in fierce combat;
I see the white fury of wave retreat,
Breaking in foam before my feet.
Then the wind tires of sport – as all must do,
And is suddenly gone – and I go too.

Sea Ride

The rock of the boat
And we're afloat
Just you and me
On a stormy sea.
She reels and she rolls
And the roll of the boat
Is almost too much to bear
But we love the whine and the wheel of the wind
And the feel of the sea in our hair.

(July 1953)

SOUTHWOLD

R.Blythe

SNAPE
ALDEBURGH

R.Alde

WOODBRIDGE
X
ORFORD

R.Deben
R.Ore
X
ORFORD
NESS

IPSWICH
X

R.Orwell

R.Stour

MANNINGTREE
HARWICH
X
Harwich Harbour

Walton
Backwaters
COLCHESTER
THE NAZE

ESSEX
WIVENHOE
WALTON-ON-THE NAZE

R.Colne
BRIGHTLINGSEA
X
CLACTON
ON SEA

MERSEA I.
WEST MERSEA

TOLLESBURY
MALDON
X
R.Blackwater
X

R.Crouch
BURNHAM ON
CROUCH

R.Roach
FOULNESS
POINT
THAMES

ROCHFORD
ESTUARY

LEIGH
SOUTHEND

SHOEBURY NESS

RIVER THAMES

SHEERNESS
NORTH
FORELAND

SHEPPEY

CHATHAM
R.Medway
WHITSTABLE
KENT
R.Swale

Roger Robinson

4

Contents

Maps and Illustrations

Front Cover. Aeolus returning home (Essex100 collection)

Other images supplied by the author or courtesy of the Essex100 collection

Sea Salt

The power of the sea
Boat tossed about
Like flotsam
Salt spray in your face

Waves knocking back
Boat leaning hard
Sails straining on the mast
Disaster one slip away

Hatches battened down
Hold on to the helm
Keep the course.
Almost there.

At last the calm
On entering the river
Wind off land, sea still
Salt drying on the bow.

Captain Paul

Introduction

For the past three years, my husband Paul and I have sailed the East coast and Suffolk rivers in our 24ft Snapdragon sailing boat *Aeolus*, moored at Stone Yacht Club on the River Blackwater. Our companions have been my brother Derek Philpott in *Gratitude* and friend Brian Little in *Sapper*, both of whom sail in Westerleys from Benfleet Yacht Club.

My friend Sheila Appleton, a local artist, suggested that I took a small notebook with me to record any poems which might occur to me as we sailed along. This I did and on my return put the poems together in a booklet. Another local artist, Penny Hawker provided the illustrations. The resulting booklet generated a lot of interest particularly among sailing friends, and many copies were sold to raise money for the Lifeboat Institute.

At the Southend Book Fair, John Debenham and Andrew Summers, co-authors of the *Essex Hundred* series of books, suggested that I develop the book further by writing about our experiences during the voyages. This I have done in the hope that the reader may experience some of the pleasure that we feel whilst sailing along these beautiful rivers.

Of course I must mention my family who have given me such support in this; my husband Paul (skipper of *Aeolus*); daughters Sally, Debbie, Jackie and her husband Paul, my son Peter and his wife Eva. They have all enjoyed our stories and poems about the sea and occasionally sailed with us to experience it all first hand. My sister, Lynda, has also given me much encouragement. A special thank you to my brother Derek to whom we owe so much of our sailing expertise, and to John and Andrew without whom this book would never have materialized.

Shirley Baker

Fair-weather Sailing

What you may ask is a 'Fair-weather Sailor' doing sitting aboard the Good Ship *Aeolus* with a 20 miles per hour wind gusting to 40 miles per hour along the River Orwell whilst 'tucked up' at Pin Mill?

'Storms never present to flurry the hulls?' Don't make me laugh. Winds can steam up with little or no warning. There is no room on a sailing boat for complacency. Of course on occasions, it could be equally dangerous if the wind should suddenly fail completely.

We have had *Aeolus* for 24 years now but before then, for 4 years, we sailed a small open dinghy. On our return from one idyllic afternoon sailing to Osea Island on the River Blackwater, the wind dropped completely and we found ourselves not moving at all, with a few miles to go before reaching home base. Darkness fell, as trying not to feel panicky, we attempted to paddle the boat along with our hands. The coast line was black showing no landmarks and we knew that under the waterline were rocks and iron spikes from old wreckages.

Then I noticed a light flashing on the shore, which I at first thought was a car head-light. Then I realised it was our teenage son, Peter, signalling with a torch. He had shown great resourcefulness to think of guiding us in and from that day I respected him as a prospective responsible adult.

Wind blowing up suddenly can have very nasty consequences. Through not fastening the hatch on *Aeolus* whilst we were on a mooring in the River Ore, on returning from a walk in Orford, we found it had completely blown off and vanished.

Aeolus is a relatively old boat, built in the 1970s on Canvey Island, Essex and we had quite a job replacing this hatch so as to remain within her character. Paul managed a makeshift solution by buying a hatch from a chandlery in Aldeburgh and adapting it to fit.

It was much smaller than our original but with the yachtsman's friend, silver duck tape, he made the gap watertight for our journey home.

We pondered for ages on how to tackle the hatch's replacement, but in the end the kind owner of an identical Snapdragon, Gemini, offered to remove his hatch so that we could prepare a pro forma and get it made up. What a friend eh?

The lesson to be learnt? Oh yes! Batten down the hatches at all times 'Fair-weather Sailors'.

Fair Weather Sailor

I could write a whole book
Of the song of the sea
Especially how pleasant it is to be
A fair weather sailor.

The sea's always calm
The sky's always blue
There's nothing daring
Or difficult to do.

You just sail along
To the laugh of the gulls
The storms never present to
Flurry the hulls.

If the forecast is good
I may sail for a day
If it's not then the answer -
I'll just stay away.

How we chose Aeolus.

For as long as I can remember, Paul wanted a sailing boat but lack of funds always kept the project away. He also wanted a boat that I too would sail in with him and enjoy. Many husbands choose boats with themselves in mind, usually very skittish and bare in comforts, then they wonder why their wives will not go sailing with them. 25 years ago, we decided that if we cashed in all our savings and took a small loan from my mother, we could just about afford one. Then we started our search for a boat.

My brother Derek that time owned a beautiful little fin keeled wooden craft named *Golden Harvest* and he took us sailing on it to see how we liked it. After our small open dinghy it seemed huge, but I am ashamed to say that as it keeled sharply over while racing along, I felt really frightened. No, this type of boat was not for me, nor with her tremendous upkeep, would it suit Paul as he was still in fulltime employment.

So we looked for a fibre glass sailing boat, one that true traditionalists would sneer at but we had to be practical. We knew nothing about the different types of boats so had to learn as we went along.

The first boat we looked at was a Hunter in a boat yard at Brightlingsea. It had a lifting keel and as I looked in the cabin I hated it on sight as it took up all the room. Then we looked round a 23 foot Snapdragon in a local creek with the delicious name of *Fair Dawn*. No head room though and you had to crawl around in her. Other boats followed suit with names as diverse as *Snoopy* and *Water Gypsy*. We were learning the whole time about the sort of boat which would finally grab us, even though we wondered if we would ever find her. One essential was for it to have 2 hatches fore and aft for adequate fire escape. We gradually narrowed it down to a Snapdragon 24 which had so many features that we both loved including nice headroom and a comfortable end cabin with 2 fair sized berths.

Now our search began in earnest. We looked in magazines, on boards outside yacht clubs and on the end of old jetties until one day at Heybridge we saw a photo of *Aeolus* who was for sale. She was out at sea at the time and Paul stood on a large rock frantically waving a newspaper to attract their attention. I think they thought we were a bit mad but eventually the owner, Brian, rowed ashore and took us out to her. I climbed aboard her  stalwart frame, and stood by her mast looking out to sea, feeling at ease and completely at home. We had found our dream. We had found *Aeolus*.

Aeolus' origins and details.

Aeolus' name comes from Greek mythology and means 'Ruler of the Winds'. An appropriate name for a boat we think. Sometimes we rub the mast and say 'Come on *Aeolus* give us a bit of a breeze'. Sometimes it works!

She was built in approximately 1971 by Thames Marine on Canvey Island, Essex, and her sail number is 86 which makes her among some of the first to be made. Her maximum sailing speed is between 6 to 7 knots but that would have to be on a very good day. It is usually around four. Her length is 24 feet and she is 8 feet 6 inches in the beam. Her draught is 2 feet 6 inches, so she can sneak along fairly shallow water such as we encounter when we sail up the twisting channel of the Alde to Snape Bridge. She has occasionally been caught out but this is usually due to lack of concentration on our behalf. Luckily we have a depth finder which beeps us if it is getting too shallow.

Head room is 5 feet 9 inches in the main cabin but a bit less in the snug. She has 5 berths, 2 in the end cabin and 3 in the dinette, but one of these is quite small. She has a separate toilet or heads as it is called.

She also has the luxury of bilge keels which means that although she is a slow boat, at night if you should sink down when the tide goes out, she stands upright and secure on her twin keels. She is made out of GRP which means that although the upkeep is still quite arduous, there is not the gruelling varnishing and care needed by a wooden yacht. Inside she has wooden panelling and a bit of brass work in her instruments and ship's clock.

Care of a fibre glass boat entails being on the look out for osmosis which can infiltrate and spoil the bodywork. This is why she comes out for a yearly check over and polish and maintenance by Paul. I help by cleaning the inside, caring for the woodwork and washing the curtains.

A Song of the Sea

A song of the sea is hard to sing
When you're on your own
And the sail's on the swing
And you're up and down
Like a coiled rubber spring
And you're all alone
In the morning.

It's easy to sing a song of the sea
When you're snug and warm
In good company
When your boat sails along
Like a proud fairee
And you're not all alone
In the morning.

Osea Island.

When time is too short for a longer cruise, we sometimes set sail for Osea Island. This was a favourite spot for us when we had our small sailing dinghy because it was so handy to step ashore, pull the boat up the beach and enjoy some nice salad and sandwiches while delighting in all the different species of birds that surround the island.

The island has a rich and varied history. It was bought in 1903 by Frederick Charrington, of the brewing family, as a retreat for recovering alcoholics. During World War Two it was a Coastal Torpedo Boat station. In 2005 it was again the site of a drug/alcohol addiction treatment centre or hospital but this was deemed unfit for use in 2010 and closed by the authorities.

Approaching the island by yacht is a unique experience. There is something about an island which arouses feelings of awe and mystery. Something to do with Robinson Crusoe I suppose. The sight of the elegant buildings surrounded by trees and shrubs has me inventing tales of their inhabitants.

It is lovely to just drop anchor and then watch the sun go down. Slowly, slowly the tide goes out leaving *Aeolus* upright on her bilge keels with only the mud and small swirling pools of water left. Of course you must remember to pass down a bucket or two for a reserve drop of water before this happens, to use as a standby, as you are now really high and dry.

Sometimes we climb down *Aeolus'* ladder in our wellies to squelch about and see the tiny creatures left in the pools. Then as the sun sets, we settle for the night until eventually the gentle sound of the water slapping against *Aeolus'* hull tells us that the tide is rising again and we can soon be on our way.

Lobster Pots and the First Sail of the Season.

When you are sailing along you must look out for lobster pots. These are a real hazard.

Often they are adequately marked by small black flags signalling as to where they lie but you must remember that they are linked together by ropes which the fisherman can pull up when required. These are fine but occasionally we find they are not so clearly marked, sometimes only by the smallest of white lozenge shaped 'fobs' which you can barely see in the waves.

We came across one set of 'fobs' on our very first sail of the season; an exceptionally fine day in May.

It was so calm and beautiful with just enough breeze to take us along. I was inspired to write my first sea poem of the year:-

It's the first sailing day of the season
And the boats are all shiny and clean
Aeolus, with barely a ripple
Sails out to see and be seen.

KERLUNK!

Paul and I looked at each other in alarm. We were just approaching Strood Creek in the River Blackwater, planning to pick up a mooring at West Mersea, then go ashore for a nice walk after lunch.

We thought at first that we had hit a sand bank and Paul tried to manoeuvre *Aeolus* forward and back to clear her out of the shallow water. It soon became obvious however that this was not the case and we were trapped by the submerged rope of some rogue lobster pots.

Using the traditional method of signalling that we were in distress, i.e. waving arms like mad to attract some attention, we were lucky that a passing fishing boat came over and after Paul had cut us loose from the thin snake-like rope that bound us, towed us to a large buoy.

Paul then took the decision to sail back to Stone and after several attempts he managed to pick up a mooring there. Our engine was completely kaput with the prop wound round with the invading rope. Luckily, with the aid of a stalwart friend at the yacht club, Roy Hall, it soon resumed working again.

Custom Officers on the River Blackwater.

I could not believe what I was seeing. We were well battened down and heading up the Blackwater to Pyefleet in the pouring rain. Paul and I were wrapped up in all our wet gear including some new bright red sou'westers and making good progress (for *Aeolus*).

There on the horizon was a Custom's Launch and it was heading our way. Surely they did not intend to stop by *Aeolus*. But they did, and swiftly drew alongside.

It was quite exciting but whatever did they want? Apart from the rain, the Blackwater looked particularly sleepy that day with no other yachts in sight.

'We want to come on board,' one of them said, quite officiously.

'Oh, would you like a cup of tea,' said I, hoping they would say 'no' as it was a bit rocky.

'No thank you,' said the officer clambering aboard. 'We want to know, have you recently crossed over from France?'

'What in this old boat – you must be joking!' I replied. Well that broke the ice. Even they could see that we were just a couple of novices out for the day in an ancient boat.

They sat having a nice chat about smuggling and such like and after about 20 minutes set off again on their way. Paul and I looked at each other and wondered why we had caused such suspicion. In the end we put it down to the large red sou'westers with their huge brims that we were wearing. Although they are marvellous in the pouring rain they are nevertheless quite conspicuous and fully hid our head and face. In a funny sort of way, we felt quite proud that we had been suspected of carrying contraband in our old *Aeolus*. It gave us a bit of 'street cred' or as my grand daughter, Zoe, would say 'Cool!' But then, it was just one of the many adventures we have had in her.

Paul's Captain's Notes - Sea mist, pre Sat-navs

When we first had *Aeolus* we sailed her round from Stone in the River Blackwater, where we kept her on a mud berth, to Two Tree Island, near Leigh-on-Sea for the winter haul out. Since we joined the Stone yacht club we have had the luxury of putting Aeolus on the hard there for the winter. One of our trips round to Leigh turned out to be "not as planned".

All necessary precautions had been taken. The weather forecast predicted a light easterly wind with the possibility of sea mist, confirmed on the 5.20am shipping forecast. Depending on the conditions the trip round can take up to 9 hours.

At two hours before low water we set off from our Stone mooring, giving us the benefit of the tide going out of the Blackwater past Bradwell and taking us down to the Wallet Spitway. There the tide would gradually change to incoming and take us down the Maplins towards the Shoebury buoys.

We were going well with the motor on as there was now no wind and the mist was getting thicker by the minute.

We listened in to the coastguard and caught a conversation with another boat which was further ahead than us. The weather forecast was given for inshore waters by the coast guard as much the same, to which the other boat indicated (not very politely) that he was in heavy fog!

The last buoy we saw was the NE Maplin, now it got really thick and we could only just see, very poorly, about ten feet in front of the bow. It was an eerie feeling! Although we plot a course on the charts and check it off, using the compass for direction and the log to tell us the speed over the water and distance travelled, one needed to see the marker buoys to confirm and back things up.

I asked Shirley to stand inside the cabin and call out the depth to me if there was any change. It soon occurred to me that as we were motoring parallel to the Maplin sands with low water in the much deeper West Swin channel, as I steered to starboard the depth fell off and when I steered to port it gradually increased. This would work right round to the Shoebury waters as well. The only problem was that we were very near the edge of the channel. The worst was when out of the gloom a wreck suddenly appeared dead ahead. By now I had got more confident and had edged up the speed. Luck was with us and there were no nasty noises as we swerved away to port.

The next thing we sighted was a large structure again dead ahead, which turned out to be Southend pier. I made a hard turn to port and avoided the pier head by a narrow margin.

The problem with the fog was that we couldn't leave our positions to check the chart or log, etc as we needed to react immediately to any change in depth or sudden obstruction.

By now we were nearly at high water so set a course for the Leigh Yacht Club moorings. Somehow we found a spare mooring and with huge relief tied up. What a strange run home it had been.

The Sea

The sea in all its many moods
Holds a fascination for me,
Sometimes it is surly, sullen and grey
Sombre in sobriety.
Sometimes it's a menacing green
A roaring treacherous foe
Fought at hard by tiny ships,
Flagging as they go.
And then it's gentle as a friend
Softly beckoning you,
The colour of it then –
A very light sunlit blue.

Essex Press Gangs

Twelve steps down to the tunnel lads
That evil lieutenant is looking for thee;
Ne'er mind you saying you've a family to keep
They want you now for the King's Navy.

To fight old Bony with Admiral Nel
You might never come back - only time will tell
But now through the tunnel you might stand a chance
When they find out there'll be a right dance.

Still you'll be safe in the old Rectory
For there the good Vicar will look after thee
Now pay me a florin for such a good tip-off
If they had got you there'd be a real rip-off.

I heard tell you could bribe them with money but then
Others could find you to start over again
They're sharpening their cutlasses ready for thee
It is such a hard life in the King's Navy.

But should you go willing, they'll give you a shilling
But is it worth it to give them your life?
Just think not to see the children again
Nor feel the caresses of your dear wife.

So down to the tunnel lads never you fear
I'll hold them off until it's all clear
I'm old and decrepit they'll never take me
I wouldn't last long in the King's Navy.

Leigh on Sea

In some ways I miss our annual sail round to Leigh on Sea. It is such an historic town, full of character and yarns about the old fishing days. The arrival of *Aeolus* in the creeks leading into Two Tree Island was somewhat of a yearly adventure. After passing by Southend Pier, full of keen fishermen casting their lines over the side looking ever hopeful for a good catch, we pass Westcliff. Soon the famous cockle sheds of Leigh come into view that attract folk from miles around to buy the delicious sea food on sale there.

Artists such as Sheila Appleton keep their studios there and produce such beautiful work which is so appreciated, not only by local people but by the many visitors to the town. There are the old pubs, such as the Peter Boat, the Crooked Billet and the Smack which could all tell yarns about smuggling if they so chose.

I consider myself lucky to live in Leigh on Sea and enjoy the many the social activities on offer. The ancient St Clements Church dominates the centre of Leigh.

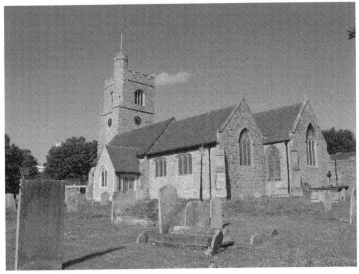

St Clements Church whose spire can be seen for miles out to sea.

Alongside is its mysterious old graveyard. Each stone tells a rich story from yesteryear. It is rumoured that a 'secret' passageway used to run from the church to the old rectory. This building was then replaced by the new Rectory, built in 1838 by the Reverend Robert Eden. It was subsequently acquired by the town council to house the Leigh Library in 1926 after the Rectory had moved to Watson House the previous year. Apparently the passage was used by men who wanted to escape the Essex Press Gangs. Today no trace of the passage way exists however twelve steps leading downwards were discovered under the church tower. Apparently the vicar used to hide male parishioners in the old rectory until the threat from the press gangs passed. It is hard to imagine such precarious times now. Still they are good to contemplate as you stand by the cobbled side road of Leigh Church to look towards the elegant red brick library, made a listed building in 1974, and feel a shiver of apprehension run through your bones!

Old Leigh still reminds us of the fishermen who used to live there with their families. Leigh Heritage Centre, in the High Street, is full of memorabilia together with the renewal of Plumbs cottage to the rear. If you wander in you can really imagine the hardship and community of those times. It has all been put together by a dedicated band of voluntary workers who still care about the history of Leigh and its preservation for the generation of today.

Landmarks at Sea

No matter which hi-tech navigational aids are owned by the skipper of any boat, in my opinion there is nothing more reassuring than a familiar land mark.

Coming out from our mooring at Stone Yacht club, we pass by the monumental Bradwell Power station, built in 1962 and decommissioned in 2002. Many people say it is an eyesore – a blot on the landscape - but for me it is a lovely solid sight and can be seen from miles away, even in a slight mist, from as far as the Wallet at Clacton-on-Sea and beyond. I always eagerly look out for it as it seems to welcome us back like an old friend.

Bradwell Power Station. A blot on the landscape?

Quite close by is another landmark, not nearly as big but one that fills you with a sense of history, as it would have been used by mariners of old. This is the tiny St Peter's Church built by St Cedd of Lindisfarne in 654 AD. It is still a place of pilgrimage and worship. Sailing along the coast you can tick off the landmarks as you see them.

There is also Clacton Pier – a defining point in the journey, followed by the significant landmark of the Walton Tower built in 1721. The sight of this lone tall structure always fills me with great excitement, for it is here that I feel the holiday has really taken off.

Clacton Pier

As you sail along, the squat Martello towers are very much in evidence. These were built at great expense around 1809 in Kent, Suffolk and Essex as a precaution should Napoleon and his fleet come sailing along our rivers with evil intent. Of the many that were built, six remain in Essex and 12 in Suffolk. Some have been converted to homes and there is one at St Osyth that has been converted to a museum. They were never used for their intended purpose of defence. Perhaps Napoleon decided not to risk sailing up our rivers when he heard about them.

Collected sayings and prayers
about the Sea

Under one of our mugs on the shelf rack is a folded piece of paper left by the previous owners. It reads:

Dear God
My boat is so very small
and thy sea so very wide
Have mercy!

A cautionary piece I keep in my diary is by the Anglo Irish dramatist J.M.Synge (1871-1909):

A man who is not afraid of the sea will soon be
drowned. For he is going out on a day he
shouldn't.
But we do be afraid of the sea, and we do only be
drowned now and again.

What a comforting thought!

Then of course, there is the sailors' hymn itself by W. Whiting (1825-78):

Eternal Father strong to save ,
Whose arm doth bind the restless wave,
Who bidds't the mighty ocean deep
Its own appointed limits keep:
Oh hear us when we cry to thee
For those in peril on the sea.

Although we are only 'fair weather sailors' there are still occasions when I have felt the need to sing this. It is not appreciated by Captain Paul though, who usually tells me, 'Not now Shirl!'

Aeolus is a comfortable, sturdy old boat. I have complete trust in her but the sea makes me realise there is another force of which we also have to take account. It is a vast force against which sometimes you must pitch your experience, skills and faith in God. At these times, remembered prayers and sayings come in handy.

May God bless her and all who sail in her!

The Wreck

I did not always look like this you know
Once I was young and full of go
Each week the captain called for me
We'd take the kids out to sea.

We'd laugh and play at pirates bold
Look for treasure, search for gold
Until they grew; found pleasures more
In keeping, than a pirate's score.

So now I'm left here to rot
My windows shattered, gone to pot.
But sometimes on the morning tide
I see again those galleons wide.

And strain my chain to take off so
To take those varmints down below.

Looking at Old Boats

There are many old boats and wrecks along this coast. To look at them sends a trigger of poignant thoughts. Thoughts of when they were prized and loved as we love *Aeolus* today. Thoughts of the boatyards who built them. Their present day sinking splendour as they gently rot down into the mud, yet still keeping their shapes.

By Pinmill on the River Orwell, many old barges have in fact been restored, some with their carcasses holding rather ramshackle homes. You can see these by taking a walk along the river path running alongside the Butt and Oyster pub.

Others like my photos taken on the walk to Sutton Hoo near Woodbridge are just sinking into oblivion their ribs barely breaking the surface as the tide rises.

Inside the Halda. Unused Copper Kettle

The most moving sight for us was an old boat named *Halda* on the hard at Walton-on-the Naze at Titchmarsh marina.

My brother could remember the boat in its hey day when he used to have coffee on board , a mere 30 years ago with its proud owners, a lovely old couple, Hal and Daphne, who had always kept her in immaculate condition. Beautiful brass window frames and wood kept varnished and gleaming.

There it lay in a neglected, sorry old state. Wood all going rotten, brass dull and grey with age. Derek nearly had tears in his eyes when he looked round her. The name plate was still in place but very faded.

One of the windows was smashed and I climbed up to look inside. Well, I wished I hadn't! A glass rack still in place with all its glasses shining and intact, even a small bottle of brandy on the shelf and a very unusual copper kettle on the lovely little stove. Talk about Miss Havisham! I felt haunted by this sight and even dreamed about it.

I'm sure there is a message there somewhere. Maybe never to put so much store on material things. I do not know.

The old couple are deceased now but their atmosphere still lingers on in that boat!

Sea Watching at Bradwell

There is something about
Looking at old worn wood
And the rotting hulks of barges
Lying leisurely on their sides

As if waiting to become
At one with the mud
Taking years to disappear
Completely - if ever

Their ribs are showing
Yet the shape of the boat
Remains; anchor chain trailing
Down into rust pool

The tide laps now
A gentle reminder of how time stalks
A boy throws stones
Into the sea.

Boats with a History

The sight of some old boats just takes your breath away when you consider their history.

I saw the lifeboat *Trimilia* moored at Woodbridge Marina in 2009. She was built by Saunders, at Cowes on the Isle of Wight, in 1925 and was sponsored by the Prudential Assurance Society. Her length is 48 feet 6 inches with a beam of 13 feet. She has been immaculately restored over the years and is now lived in by her owner and his wife. Such luxurious living accommodation which was maintained so beautifully made my jaw drop open in amazement.

The history of the *Trimilia* is also quite remarkable. In the war time she was one of the famous Dunkirk boats that helped to save thousands of lives. Her owner today has photos and names of the men she saved. It was my pleasure to hear him speak about her with such pride.

In Ipswich Neptune Marina we saw the *Dowager* lifeboat, previously named *Rosa Wood* and *Phyllis*. She made three trips to Dunkirk and saved 143 lives.

Dowager of London

I read her plaque about how the Naval Officer in charge had built a makeshift wheel house to protect his men from shrapnel.

There is something about these Dunkirk boats that brings a lump to my throat. The bravery of ordinary sailors was outstanding in times of such awfulness and hardship. We must never forget them.

Another sighting on land at Ipswich Marina, was Herman Goering's old sailing boat, *Marabou,* which was seized by the British Navy after World War II. In 1952 the *Marabou* took part in the 1,400 mile Bermuda to Plymouth race and was skippered by Keith Frank Rogerson from Hereford. At the time of our sighting the vessel had not been restored but nevertheless you could only gaze at the superb graceful lines of its hull and its torn sign, *Marabou,* in wonder. The vessel was returned to Germany in 2011.

From Southend to Brightlingsea

Derek and Brian keep their boats, *Gratitude* and *Sapper*, at Leigh on Sea and meet up with us for our annual sailing holiday. They sail down the Thames and past the Maplins to join us at Brightlingsea or Pyefleet Creek to commence our trip.

The early morning shipping forecast has to be listened to carefully before they can make their plans. They do not proceed if the wind is a strong north easterly as they have to negotiate passage through some very narrow channels. Also if the wind is north easterly the sea will be extremely rough due to the wind blowing against the tide.

The distance from Southend to Brightlingsea is thirty nautical miles. If the boats arrive at the Southend pier by high water, the South Whittaker Buoy just south of the River Blackwater, twenty nautical miles distant, can be achieved in five hours taking advantage of the outgoing tide. With an easy sail of minimum speed of three and a half knots this is not a problem (1 knot is 1.15 statute miles or 1.85 km.).

Passing the West Shoebury Starboard Buoy

Derek and Brian do their best to keep the Maplin Sands (the Government firing range) well to port. If you are detected as being too close, you will get a warning call from Shoe Radar. Keeping course can sometimes be tricky as it is very narrow at the West Barrow sand bank to starboard and even at low water sand banks can be awash.

The two vessels will pass the South Whittaker buoy, close to port, all the while heading north to the Swin Spitway (Wallet). They then go through the gap between the Buxey Sand and the Gunfleet Sand as shown on the Thames Estuary chart.

It is really essential charts are kept up to date as the sand banks are liable to move, especially the one named 'The Wallet'.

From here it is 10 nautical miles to Brightlingsea. No short cuts are taken until the Colne Bar is rounded to starboard. Then it is 345 degrees to the Brightlingsea Beacon.

If good time has been made on the above run and it is a low tide, they would be unable to get into the entrance at Brightlingsea. The alternative is to proceed to Pyefleet Creek where they can either drop anchor or pick up a mooring.

However if the wind was south westerly, Derek and Brian would have had an

Almost there

excellent sail. It is interesting to note that in addition to modern markers and buoys, there are still many man made markers left there from 200 years ago. Research has shown that there may have been forests on the Maplin sands many years ago. It is said the ancient Nordic invaders first concealed their raiding fleets in this area.

The Little Ships
of Leigh
May 1940

Defender, Endeavour, Letitia,
Reliant, Renown and Resolute:-

Were the little ships sent from Leigh
They had to join 800 more
To sail to Dunkirk's distant shore
And change a course of history.

The convoy sailed past Margate pier
Their course set firm and true
The treacherous Channel surf died down
As if to help the bawleys through.

A shallow slope led to the beach
Not unlike the one at Leigh
But this one was under fire
From the Wehrmacht enemy.

300,000 men were trapped
And so the gallant fleet
Moved in to lift them from the sands
Out to a deeper reach.

The Renown was blasted by a mine
And all her crewmen died
A memorial stone stands by Leigh Church
To tell their names with pride.

'Greater Love hath no man than this.
That a man lay down his life for his friends.'

36

Red Sands Army Fort

You encounter a strange man-made sight as you sail past the Maplins on the way to Leigh-on-Sea. It is the *Red Sands* army fort. Its location is seven nautical miles north of Whitstable and three nautical miles south east of the Black Tail Spit buoy in the River Thames.

These constructions loom out at sea like huge squarish static robots. During the war, however, they formed a crucial part of our defence. They are one of many such structures to be found around the coast and were designed by Guy Maunsell in 1941.

Red Sands army fort consists of five anti air-craft towers surrounding a central and radar tower. They are one of several forts built in the Thames in 1943, such as the Nore and Shivering Sands forts.

Although they were built over 60 years ago, it is reported that they are still in fair condition, considering they have been open to the elements all this time.

Pirate Radio Stations soon found them to be a good place to set up and operate from. In 1964, the *Shivering Sands* fort was occupied by Screaming Lord Sutch's *Radio Sutch* and the Red Sands fort was used by Radio *Invicta*.

Invicta closed in 1965 after a tragedy occurred when three men, Tom Pepper, D.J. Simon Ashley and engineer Martin Shaw, all drowned when their boat *David* sank on route to Faversham.

After 1965, *Red Sands* fort started transmitting again, this time calling itself *King Radio*. This was run by John Thompson and five other business men. Unfortunately its signal was too weak to attract potential advertisers and the station soon ran into financial difficulties.

The army forts were originally constructed by first class engineers in strict accordance with Guy Maunsell's instructions. You could say that these structures were the precursors of the present day oil rigs.

Red Sands is at present under threat of demolition because it could be classed as a potential danger to the nearby shipping lane. However, a group of enthusiasts are hoping to keep it going as an historical monument.

Without a doubt the sight of these old forts looming up out at sea, whilst sailing peacefully in *Aeolus*, brings back many nostalgic memories of the pirate radio days of the 1960s.

Shivering Sands Fort, former home of Radio Sutch and Radio City

Seals

Sometimes at sea you come across a sight that is so unbelievably beautiful it takes your breath away. Such a sight for Paul and I one day was when were sailing along in *Aeolus* and saw a seal happily sunning itself on a sandbank.

It looked so happy, so at peace, blissfully surveying the passing ships as if it had all the time in the world. Its round 'puppy dog' face and large eyes were absolutely captivating. It was quite large and seemed so incongruous as it lay there.

Seals can be spotted along the River Crouch between Foulness and Potton Island, indeed there are special excursions which can take visitors to see them. But we had the unexpected sight of this one as we approached Pyefleet Creek on the Blackwater. There are many different types of seal, the grey and common seal favouring the Essex Coast.

Our seal looked so sleek and well fed, positively preening itself in the sun. Information on the web reveals that after weaning they are soon off to make their own way in the world, returning home after around five years to mate.

An interesting note about their mating habits is that they all give birth at the same time due to their practice of delayed implantation. How sensible is that! We certainly felt privileged to see this special creature.

Ode to a Seal

Oh Seal
How happy you are
Big deal
There on your sand bank
Surveying us all
As we pass by.
Fat and sleek
Wisdom beaming
From your large eyes
What a surprise
To see you there.
Don't mind if we stare
We are not used
To seeing
Such a natural creature
Being so content
With what life has to offer.

40

Tollesbury Marina

If you have lively youngsters with you a good place to visit is Tollesbury Marina. Derek often puts in here with his very active grandsons, Ben aged 11 and Ethan aged 9.

For a start it is right next to a sheltered beach should you wish to swim in the sea. It also has its own undercover swimming pool and tennis courts too. How handy is that!

There are 250 berths there with water and electricity. Lovely meals can be obtained at the Cruiser Club restaurant which is open to visitors and so handy for planning a reunion or group sail.

It was founded in 1970 by enthusiasts and opened officially in 1971. It has a tidal harbour where you can arrive for two hours on either side of high water. From Nass Beacon, you follow the red and green cans westward to Tollesbury. At the entrance to Woodrolfe Creek is a tide gauge marking the height of the tide over the sill, so obviously you must not enter until you have sufficient water to clear. Should you arrive late, there are some lit buoys to help you.

Tollesbury is at the mouth of the river Blackwater, so it is an ideal spot for *Aeolus* to sail to because it is so close to Stone yet offers a lovely weekend break. It is also the perfect gateway to Holland, Belgium and France should you be an adventuresome sailor.

On arrival it is pleasant to dawdle into the village and look round at this and that. There is a reasonable small café near the sail lofts. Very relaxing! The village of Tollesbury has a fascinating history but you have to look for it. It used to be known as the Plough and Sail village as at one time all local livelihoods were obtained either from agriculture or the sea or both.

A sight which always fascinates me are the four old sail lofts on the right hand side of the walk in. They are distinctive wooden buildings with ladders reaching up to the first floor.

They have been built on stilts and were built in the early 1900s. Later they were used for the winter storage of sails from the J class yachts. In the 1930s the local fishermen would leave their fishing occupation in the summer to race the 120 ft long yachts in the Mediterranean. These must have been such exciting times for them. Now the lofts are the offices for local boat yards.

The reason for the stilts is that when the high spring tides come the land becomes covered in water, even though the lofts are a quarter of a mile from the waterside. This caught Derek out one day as he returned from shopping in the village, only to find he was cut off from returning to the Marina.

Behind the sail lofts is the retired Porthcawl Light Ship. This imposing looking red ship was previously stationed on the south coast of Wales in the 60s and 70s, to warn against the nearby sand bank of Scarweather. She finished her duties in 1988 and was renamed Trinity. It was acquired by a Christian organization called the Fellowships Afloat Charitable Trust for children's activity holidays.

The Porthcawl Lightship

Tollesbury used to be serviced by a railway from Kelvedon to Tollesbury pier called the Crab and Winkle line. It was authorized under a Light Railway Order on the 29th January, 1901 and much celebration took place when it was finished in October, 1904. One hundred and twenty guests made the first run to Tollesbury. Despite the original   high hopes of local business men, including Mr Arthur Wilkin of Tiptree Jam fame, the Crab and Winkle line closed in May, 1951. The Tollesbury Pier fell into disrepair and the floods of 1953 finally washed it away.

There is so much to see and ponder over at Tollesbury. The old church of St. Mary's dating from the 11th century is well worth a visit. It used to be owned by St Mary's nunnery, part of Barking Abbey, which was dissolved in 1539 by Henry VIII.

Due to the fact that there were quite a few pubs at Tollesbury, of which only two remain, one gathers it was not always the quiet place it seems today. This comes over when you read the words on the font of the Church:

'Good People all I pray take care
That in ye Church you doe not sware.'

In 1718 a fine was imposed on a Mr John Norman for doing so.

Should you not want to even think about historical facts, the sight of these Essex salt marshes, rich in pink and purple sea lavender, may take your breath away. There are of course the coast loving birds, waders, golden plovers, egret, reed warblers, lesser black backed gulls, hen and marsh harriers and short eared owls to watch out for.

Oh yes, 'quiet' Tollesbury has something to offer for everyone. That is why *Aeolus* will be sailing there again very soon.

Pyefleet Creek

There is something about this creek which stirs my imagination. Did pirates once sneak in here with their contraband goods before setting off along the mainland?

It is known for its superb anchorage, especially near the old oyster shed where you can remain afloat at low tide. Sometimes you can pick up a mooring but must be prepared to pay for this in the height of the season, or even move off if the owner returns. It is best to examine the rope of the mooring to see if sufficient weed suggests a long absence of use.

It is an ideal spot to meet up with our sailing companions, my brother Derek on *Gratitude* and friend Brian on *Sapper* who both sail round from Leigh-on-Sea. Within sight of Brightlingsea, we feel that the holiday is about to commence.

Sometimes Paul and I row ashore and go for a pleasant walk along the sea wall to Cudmore Park. This is a lovely open spot where children enjoy flying their kites and having picnics. There is an excellent little information office there where hot drinks and ice cream can be bought. Also there are toilets.

For those who like to consider the history of the place, if you walk back along the beach you can see earth banks of an old fort operational in the 16th and 17th century in defence of the River Colne.

It is also a good place to see sailing barges as they sometimes drop anchor at the mouth of the river. Now there are only a few left but in their heyday there were hundreds of them and must have looked an amazing sight as they gently sailed by, blending in with the soft colours of the Essex countryside.

Withies at Pyefleet Creek

The sapling holds
Dried twig branches to the sky.
Destined to grow and flourish
From its extended form.

Now a thing of warning
Withered in permanence
A sign of stark reality
Watched for by sailors.

Its base in lapping water
And no birds singing
In leafy branches
Just the scream of gulls.

Ghost like echoes
Of a living past.

The use of *withies* is an old traditional method of marking
the minor tidal channels in our harbours and estuaries still
in use today. They are made of willow and stuck in the mud
to show where the deeper water lies.

Barges

Anyone who loves the sea must surely be moved by the sight of Thames Sailing Barges on the water. We have been so lucky to see these magnificent craft go sailing by as we sit on *Aeolus* on our deep water mooring at Stone.

An event which is so exciting to watch is the Sailing Barge Match along the River Blackwater. In 2010, this event took place in July, but the date does vary from year to year.

The Sailing Barge Association has a website which is very informative and gives the names of barges in alphabetical order, along with their accompanying photographs and histories. We sit at home in winter, scrolling up these delicious details which in turn makes us yearn for the summer to come quickly. The Barges have wonderful names such as *Lady Daphne of Rochester* or simply *Will of London*. Many of them were built between the 1890s and early 1920s. However, their origins go back long before that. One can only guess at the amount of hard work and dedication that goes into their restoration and upkeep.

The early barges were mainly open craft with only one square sail but later they were fitted with decks and hatch covers for their one large hold. The newer barges carried a sprit sail rig which is one of the oldest types of fore and aft rigging used since the Roman times. Most of the rigs are similar consisting of a large sail placed well forward on the vessel. They carry around 4000 square feet of sail which have distinctive reddy brown colouring.

Barges are flat bottomed which makes them ideal for loading at low tide, especially in and around the Thames Estuary. The barges were constructed for easy handling by a minimum of crew. The craft are usually made of English oak and often have stayed within the same family for years, with all sailing skills being passed down from father to son.

The first sailing matches were introduced by William Dodd in 1863, when barges were not only built to carry cargo but also for speed and also to enhance the prestige for the owners.

Some barges were used for smuggling especially those which carried hay. They were stacked very high. Illicit goods could easily be hidden once offloaded onto the barges from ships arriving from abroad. Although many of the barges slipped though the customs without suspicion, should they be caught the penalties were severe. As a punishment for the owner, a barge would be sawn in two. How drastic is that!

When you think of the early 20th century and the horse traffic in London, hay and straw were in much demand. Hay would be picked up from the farms at Canvey, Benfleet, Foulness, and others along the Rivers Crouch, and River Blackwater. There is so much to learn about the barges. However  for Paul and I, we are simply content to watch the lovely procession of sailing vessels passing us as they race. We can only marvel at their continued existence.

The Boat

The boat in the shallow creek;
     Grandfather's sinewy arms, creaking oars,
small boy dreaming.

The boat anchored by the bank;
     wide-brimmed hats, thermos flask, sandwiches.

The boat in the small boy's dream;
     Custom officers, contraband, skull and crossbones.

The boat forgotten; the boy's a man now,
     Bride, confetti, children, mortgage.

The boat neglected; barnacles slime and leaking water.
     Grandfather's coffin, flowers and hymn books.

The boat discovered found in a boat yard;
     worked on at weekends, ladders, varnish.

The boat restored:
     out at sea, dancing on her mooring,
          waiting for the man…

Brightlingsea

This is one of my favourite stopping places. I think it lives up to its name, a really bright little town by the sea. It lies close to the mouth of the Colne at its meeting with the River Blackwater and the Thames estuary. Sailing past the red and green buoys leading into the harbour, we just know that we are in for a really nice welcome from the Harbour Master as we call him on the radio (Channel 68). If you can tell him what time you hope to arrive he will, if at all possible, give you a guiding and helpful hand. Of course he may be busy, in which case you have to find a temporary spot and wait for further instructions.

It is such a lovely feeling to glide past the lines of secured yachts, looking at their names and different shapes and sizes and thinking, *Aeolus* soon will be one of their number.

It has not always been so civilised to tie up at Brightlingsea. Some years ago, before the smart pontoons were in place, there was a system of two poles with a rising ring holding a chain. First *Aeolus* needed to be secured to one pole, then it was necessary to nip smartly aft to secure the other before the boat had a chance to slew out into the river.

On one occasion, I was holding on midships to the stays of another yacht while Paul quickly rowed round in our dinghy to tie up the other end of the boat. He then ignored his own instructions of 'always stand in the middle of the boat'. The whole lot toppled over and poor Paul landed in the murky water. Now the challenge was for me to hold on despite *Aeolus* drifting rapidly away. Ever felt as if you were going to be pulled in half? Luckily Paul managed to get back into the dinghy and save the day!

If you arrive in the high season, from Thursday to Saturday, you can call up a launch and have the luxury of being taken to shore. (Radio 37 or M1).

If not, it is no hardship to row in and tie up by the side of the hammer head of the private jetty belonging to Colne Yacht Club.

Peaceful times at Brightlingsea

Once on shore, there is so much to see; the quaint winding streets with some of the old houses built for fishermen, the friendly pubs and of course the charity shops. Then there are the most tempting smells emanating from the famous fish and chip shop near the quay itself. It is such a pleasure to sit on one of the nearby benches whilst eating supper and looking out to sea.

There is little trace of the anxious times of the 1990's when the inhabitants had to battle to stop live animals being sent for export from this harbour.

Little Dog in a Lifejacket at Brightlingsea

Little dog in a life jacket
 Your mistress takes no chances
 She loves you very much
 And you lead her merry dances.

 You have to be taken for a walk
No matter sun or rain
 And if you tumble overboard
 You're hoisted up again.

There's a special handle on your suit
 To grab then tie a line
 And now I come to think of it
 It's better far than mine!

Sand Turtle at Pyefleet

Decorated by sea weed
And oyster shells

Feet moulded
Imprinted with toes

Blue mussels
Marking toe-nails

Creature lovingly formed
By children

Patted and shaped
Laughed at

Left with backward glances
Of pride

Firmly placed in their memory
Before destruction

By incoming
Waves

Greedy elements
Of wind and sea.

Historical Brightlingsea.

Paul and I often have a good walk whilst in Brightlingsea and one of the places we are thrilled to visit is the church on the hill, All Saint's Church. It was built in 1250. On our most recent visit we went inside to see the magnificent building. It was very impressive, but particularly striking for me were the kneelers made in tapestry. Such a lot of work and love must have gone into the making them. Even from the church's grounds there are very commanding views overlooking the countryside and the sea. Unfortunately the church is not always open due to surveillance problems.

From Brightlingsea, we have used our fold-up bikes to cycle to Dedham although it did take us all day. It was worth it though to see the glorious Constable countryside.

Brightlingsea is a liberty of the Cinque port of Sandwich in Kent. At one time it was an island. This is not hard to picture as when the tide goes out you can see the rivulets all around leaving large areas of exposed land. When walking through the town, we always stop to marvel at an extremely old house, Jacob's House. Its front faces the sea so you are actually looking at the rear of the property which is over 600 years old. You can really let your imagination run away with you here as you reach for your guidebook.

A sea walk takes us past the beach huts. These are so ideal for families looking for a day by the sea with the simple pleasures of paddling and digging in the sand. Nearby is Bateman's tower. It was put up by Mr Bateman in 1883, believing the air would be beneficial to his daughter who had contracted T.B. Lottery money has enabled its distinctive roof to be restored.

One of the delights of Brightlingsea is 'Brightlingsea in Bloom'. The sight of this event always takes my breath away when this little town is just awash with marvellous floral decorations.

53

Hanging baskets, tubs, old rowing boats and any container that you can think of will be dripping with the most gorgeous displays of flowers. It is as if every person living there is just bursting with pride at what a small town can achieve with volunteers and a little sponsorship. They have justly won many gold medals and competitions.

It is one of our main pleasures of the year just to see it and be there.

Wind Turbines at Sea

We are so used to seeing wind turbines on the land, it gave us a mild shock to see them when sailing on *Aeolus* rounding into the Blackwater from the River Colne.

Here are these bland white creatures gently rotating their monster arms out at sea. They have been built on sand banks on many sites along the Thames estuary and Essex coast. Apparently the coastal wind force is far greater than inland. It would be, when you stop to think about it, because it is so flat out at sea, there is no restriction. However I could not help staring as though hypnotized by the sight of these objects. For a start, it must be far dearer to erect such a thing at sea. Not only do they appear in these beloved local rivers, but also in the North Sea where there are many seemingly floating windmills.

I started daydreaming about what would happen should a storm blow up and *Aeolus* be drawn into their circle of sorcery. But then, I am just a poet on a sailing boat. It is a good job that Paul and my companions are much more practical.

PS

On the 19th January 2011, I read an account in the Daily Telegraph, that despite wind farms being praised by our politicians, last year the wind farms turned less in 2010 due to there being less wind around now. Oh no! Don't say these intrusive structures are blotting our land and seascapes for nothing! We will have to watch this space!!

Wind Turbines

Bland white ladies arms turn round
Embracing the wind but firm in the ground
Turning , turning, hypnotize
Strange creatures there before our eyes.
In a circle, mystic so
Do not lure our ships below.

Some Practical Information

Beaufort wind scales

Beaufort Number	mean velocity knots	descriptive terms
0	1	calm
1	1-3	light breezy
2	4-6	ditto
3	7-10	gentle breeze
4	11-16	mod breeze
5	17-21	fresh breeze
6	22-27	strong breeze
7	28-33	near gale
8	33-40	gale
9	41-47	strong gale
10	48-55	storm
11	56-63	violent storm
12	64 +	hurricane

1 Knot = 1.15 statute miles or 1.85km

You can listen to the weather forecast on the Radio on:
00.48hrs or 05.20hrs Long Wave and FM

And Long Wave only
12.01 hrs and 17.54 hrs.

Modern mobile phones enable you to obtain the latest inshore waters weather forecast at any time.

Thunderstorm

The thunderstorm
Rumbles round the sky
My craft is small
And we're well shut in.

Good books to read
And yarns to tell
Coffee to brew
And all is well.

After the Storm

After steep waves
        the joy of the calm

after strong winds
        a breeze's balm

after thundering skies
        a sunset bright

a safe harbour for me
        to rest the night.

Wet Gear

So you've pulled on your wellies
Heaved up your salopettes
Positioned the shoulder straps
Under your wets.

Zipped up the zipper
On oilskin and fleece
Pulled up the hood
And stepped onto deck

Turned to face the rain
And ongoing debris;
And then comes that feeling
You now want to pee.

Sailing Snippet

This isn't the time for sailing
Rather to sit at the back of the boat
To watch the gulls and the sea
And send text messages to friends.

'Good Books to Read'

When *Aeolus* is moored up or at anchor in the evening, out come the books. These are some that I have loved.

The Kite Runner and *A Thousand Splendid Suns* –Khaled Hosseini
Shadow of the Wind - Carlos Ruiz Zafon
The Life of Josephine Bonaparte by Sandra Gulland (3 volumes – could last the entire trip!)
The Book Thief-Marcus Zusak
The *Lady Detective* stories of McCall Smith.
The Yorkshire Dale school inspector-Gervais Phinn.
The House at Riverton -Kate Morton
The Dig by John Preston (great if you are near Sutton Hoo!)
Mr Pip by Lloyd Jones
The Island and *The Return* -Victoria Hislop
The Rose of Sebastopol - Katherine McMahon
The Memory Keeper's Daughter - Kim Edwards
Salmon Fishing in the Yemen - Paul Torday.
The Essex Hundred. A Poetic history of Essex. This book includes a poem on the Walton Tower for me, the outstanding land mark we see as we head round the coast.

All of these have been my companions on our voyages and I recommend them for a really good read. I am always on the look out for good offers from book shops, or of course, the charity shops where you can buy a good book for a few pence. I never take library books – as I would worry all the time that they might be dropped in the water.

Titchmarsh Marina

I find it so exciting to sail along the Walton Backwaters and think about how they inspired author Arthur Ransome's story called *Secret Waters*. Somehow you can imagine the adventures taking place there. Sometimes we pick up a mooring and look around us in a sort of reverie.

Sailing into Titchmarsh Marina following the instructions of a very helpful staff is a real pleasure. Here you can enjoy a few days civilized sojourn. There is everything a visiting yachtsman could wish for. There are clean showers, a good shop, an interesting little walk round in the evening looking at the boats on the hard and a first class restaurant should you have tired of self catering.

It is a fair walk to Walton on the Naze itself, however time soon passes with good company chatting away and before you know it, you will have walked the couple of miles! On the way there is much to look at. I even find the many different caravan parks fascinating. At Walton church there is a bus stop should you wish to venture further along the coast or inland. Walton train station is also nearby.

In the grounds of All Saints' Church, built in 1896, is a memorial made of three blades of a Halifax propeller that commemorates the brave Canadian crew who were shot down over the sea in 1945. We always pause to look at this memorial. Even today occasionally flowers are left as a mark of respect.

The Church has had subsidence problems that have caused cracking to the building. The Church is currently endeavouring to raise funds to help deal with this.

Another church at Walton built in medieval times sank into the sea without trace. Sometimes bells are said to be heard from where it used to stand. We all love a spooky tale and sometimes we stand by to contemplate this rumour. However, only the sounds of the waves were heard by us. Perhaps if you visit and listen closely you will here more.

The main attraction for me is Walton Tower. It is such a wonderful beacon and has such a remarkable history. Please also see page 67.

It is invigorating to walk along the seafront past the holiday sites. Along this front, prehistoric sharks' teeth have been found. Some of them are for sale in the local curio shop. There are many interesting little shops to look in but at the time of writing there is no bank.

If you choose to walk in the opposite direction you come across the neat little seaside town of Frinton. This community has really guarded its quiet position. Just outside the town there is a new shopping arcade which is a delight to look round.

Oh yes, *Aeolus*, *Sapper* and *Gratitude* have enjoyed many a pleasant few days here at Titchmarsh and with luck will do so again. Another bonus is that it is so easy to get on and off the boat with the well thought out pontoons. You can if you wish take your bikes with you and explore the town on two wheels.

Line up of boats at Titchmarsh

SAPPER, KOKOMO, SWILLY PIG 11,
FAWLTY PYTHON
SWIFT, PRIDE OF ORWELL

OPTIMIST, AEOLUS, SHINDY 1V
FREE SPIRIT, TITANIA, HASSLE

PHAEDRA of SEAFORD, ARABELLA
CARPE DIEM, LILIAN M, GRATITUDE

Sailing with Animals.

I am full of admiration for sailing folk who take their pets with them out to sea. We have seen quite a few pets on boats and I have to say that, in the main, they look very content with their lot and seem to have adapted well to their sea lives, in some cases better than visiting human beings.

Of course, the owners consider their welfare carefully. Ideally dogs should wear a life jacket in case they fall into the water. They should also be taken for a daily walk if at all possible. Some pontoons are made of metal mesh and are quite hard for padded feet to walk on. This is a problem when the owner leaves the boat, for the dog has either to be carried or put on a trolley.

I saw a very unusual dog on board a sailing boat at Titchmarsh Marina. It was a black long haired Newfoundland dog and to my eyes she looked like a small bear. Her name was Kate and her owner told me that her breed came from Canada. The dog was bred to help the fishermen in icy waters. It is the reason why they have thick oiled coats which keep out the cold and they have webbed feet to help them swim.

Her fur had to be regularly trimmed so she would not get too hot in the summer. Kate did not seem perturbed by her surroundings and sat on deck, with her lead secured round the mast, serenely surveying all the boats around her. I had never seen a dog like this before. Despite her size, she seemed very gentle especially when the grandchildren came to visit. I was later told that one of these dogs had saved his master's life when he had fallen in the sea whilst fishing in Scotland. What an amazing breed they are! Even so, the thought of one on board *Aeolus* would be too much for me to contemplate!

Another unusual dog belonged to a friend of my brother's, Roy, at Leigh Yacht club. She was a Border Collie named Bonnie and we met her whilst sailing to Brightlingsea.

She was such a useful pet. She had the ability to round up the children, no doubt using all her herding instincts. However she did have one little anomaly in that she loved to go wind surfing with Roy sitting behind him on his board, looking as if she was so enjoying the experience of the wind on her face. What a strange sight she looked as they surfed together on the sea at Leigh and elsewhere. Her sport was curtailed however when a 'well wisher' informed the RSPCA who then deemed it was cruel. Roy was forbidden to take her anymore. Bonnie howled in protest and had to be physically restrained when Roy took off without her!

One story of a pet at sea stands out above the rest. This is the story of the cat 'Jon Boy', a Turkish Van who was rescued from a cattery after a car accident. After the accident the owner no longer wanted him. Jon Boy had the beautiful colouring of the Vans, whitish body fur and a ginger tail.

Apparently Jon Boy "wrote" an annual account of his sailing adventures on his new owner, Ian Kemp's, yacht *Breeze*, a Spray 36! Ian has given me permission to record some of his writings which appeared in the Leigh Yacht Club's magazine, *Cockleshells*. The following advertisement, appeared following the demise of a cat, called Lucifer.

Live in Cat Wanted

A position has become vacant due to the death of the previous resident. We require a cat who is sociable, good tempered, adaptable and willing to travel. He will be responsible for on board pest control and other routine duties. Apply via our Agent, Messrs Woodland Cattery.

Jon Boy tells how he applied to be the ship's cat:

'I was in lodgings at the time and this advertisement came to my notice and I thought I may as well apply. I really did not know what this 'yacht' business was but it had to be an improvement on my present situation'.

Jon Boy later he writes:

'I was always under the assumption that this job as 'Ship's Cat' was a bit of a doddle. I wouldn't tell the Skipper that since he expects a proper job all the time being as he is a retired ship's captain. However all you have to do really is to look busy hunting around for things and chasing seagulls off the deck and he is happy enough.'

2002 was a dramatic year at sea for Jon Boy as he fell overboard! He records this in his special cat way:

'Have you ever tried swimming in November? I can't say that I would recommend it and it's salty and tastes awful!'

Luckily for his master and the readers of his column, he managed to climb up a piece of heavy rope and scamper up onto a nearby barge. Jon Boy wrote for the magazine from 2000 until 2008 and I am sure he was loved by all his readers. It seems to me that the owners of pets at sea are a special breed in themselves, and the pets that accompany them can be true sailing companions.

A Fault Rectified (from Captain's notes)

Although *Aeolus* has been the perfect boat for us, over the years we became troubled by an annoying trait of the engine. It would not start when hot. Most diesel engines have a problem starting from cold, hence the cans labeled 'cold start' in the chandler's shops. We received much friendly advice from friends. 'It needs bleeding,' said one. He showed Paul the intricacies of bleeding the fuel from the low pressure pipe into the fuel injector pump until no air bubbles were seen. This was followed by the same procedure on the high pressure side on the delivery valve holder, and finally the injector itself. Bingo, we thought, the problem was solved.

But alas, it was not to be. The engine started from cold from the first stroke but if it was hot the only way was to give it a squirt of 'cold start'. We then had a top overhaul carried out. This involved the engine head being removed for the valve seatings to be checked and ground down to obtain the best compression. This did improve hot starting for the rest of the season but over the years things went gradually back to how they were before.

A second overhaul indicated there was nothing wrong. We decided that the fuel injector valve needle was worn down and Paul undertook the replacement. When trying it out, it did seem to be a success but just as Paul was beginning to feel smug that all was well, he realized that the engine was very slowly increasing in revs. The throttle did not seem to have any effect. Realizing that the engine was out of control and going faster and faster, he had a mad scramble for the correct spanner to unscrew the fuel connection to the injector valve. We have since learned that this is a known problem when setting up the engine. We gave a huge sigh of relief when she started. Things were back to normal. (To this day we have a correct size injector spanner to hand, so far never used.)

After a few years the problem of hot starting returned and was worse than ever so a local engineer was called in. He decided that the fuel pump was not delivering when the engine was hot, so it was replaced but it only made a slight improvement in hot starting. We were not out of the woods yet!

The next year, a routine visual check whilst at Ramsholt on the River Deben, revealed that no water was coming out of the rear and the engine was overheating. This indicated that the water impellor was not working. On replacing the water impellor, things were back to 'normal', i.e. starting first time cold but not starting when hot. At this point despair was setting in. Perhaps the only solution was to get a new engine at great cost.

However help came from an unexpected source. Booking in to the Titchmarsh marina, Paul noticed that they had an engineer from 'French Marine' in residence and decided to give the problem one last try. He agreed to have a look. After checking out the engine and listening to our sorry tale, he indicated that unless the adjustment on the fuel injector was fully open on starting it would give problems. He then checked and re-set it and we could hardly believe that this would do the trick. However, it started up hot and subsequently the engine runs perfectly.

Hot, cold or indifferent, 'Boom!' the engine starts first time. Somehow Paul thinks that this was the problem all along.

We just needed a man that knew. (Fingers crossed!)

The Heart of a Boat

The heart of a boat is its engine
The soul of a boat is its sail
The mind of a boat is its captain
Holding fast through the oncoming gale.

The friends of a boat are the sea gulls
Who scream with encouraging glee
The foes of a boat are the grey hard rocks
That lie in the depths of the sea.

The captain's friend is the compass
Which shows him the way to go
Following lines on the good ship's chart
To put him in the know.

The captain's joy is the harbour
All safe from storm and harm
Hot coffee brewing on the stove
Will add to the cabin's charm.

Walton Tower

Through the mist we see you now
A column of unchanging certainty
WaltonTower blesses us in our sights
As we sail hard across the sea.

Over 'Prebenda Consumpta' we come
Oh can we hear those sunken bells?
Well hidden now beneath the sea
And only in tales that history tells.

The coffins floated back to land
To be caught by villagers waiting there
And many a table, many a chair
Were fashioned on shore by eager hands.

We may not hear the bells that tolled
Nor see the smugglers secret works
But know full well the waves that rolled
Helped them in their shameful perks.

So now we've sailed the Northern Sea
And safely we've come home
Guided by that Walton Tower
We'll rest before we roam.

But after, we will cast off again
Through Backwaters find our way
The battle calls us and we'll fight
Through many another day.

Yacht Clubs.

It is quite a good idea to belong to a yacht club. For many years Paul and I were 'loners'. However we now appreciate the practical help the club can give you such as taking the boat out of the water for the winter. There is a great feeling of comradeship, such as at the annual dinner, with endless yarns over the non events of the previous season when bad weather has stopped the more feeble of us venturing forth. Then of course there is friendly advice on hand for essential winter maintenance and help returning the boat to water in the early summer. There is also the hospitality offered from members of one yacht club to another. This means that you can arrive at a club as a visiting yachtsman and be offered their facilities such as showers, meals and drinks at the bar if you sign their visitors' book.

Many yacht clubs have a fascinating history. My brother, Derek, belongs to both Leigh Sailing Club and Benfleet Yacht Club and investigations have shown that the former was established in the 1890's when the Bawleys used to race as a class at the annual regatta. The yacht club premises ranged from being part of Admiral Haddock's house in Leigh, to *Veronica,* a floating HQ from 1922 until 1937. This was followed by the *Lady Quirk* and other boats including the *Raymond* with their fine old histories.

After 1948 they held their meetings at the Crooked Billet. In the 1960's Leigh old railway station was converted by the members to become their new club house.

Our own club at Stone also has an interesting history. Stone was the home to motor torpedo boats during the war. They were busy hunting down German craft on patrol in the Channel. In 1944, Stone became a naval supply base and supported the construction of the Mulberry harbours and then allied forces in France.

Although the clubs are there for our mutual enjoyment of the sea, I find their histories are really facinating.

A Bee at Sea (Passing Clacton Pier)

Amazing to see
A bee at sea
This little bumbling thing
Rotating wing
Pays you a visit

Flies around mast
And fore and aft
Does he need a rest
After so many miles?
Not he. Not he.

For he is the amazing bee
The amazing buzzing bumbling bee.

Bees are the most amazing creatures. Whenever one pauses to rest its fat little body on *Aeolus* half way across the river, I am filled with awe.

For a start, in proportion to its body, its wings seem so gossamer like and tiny. Then the way they work by using a rotating action seems incredible. Sometimes they rest for a few minutes, sometimes a few hours, accepting *Aeolus'* gentle sounds and movements as we sail over the waters.

The more bees are studied the more incredible facts become known about them. The latest discoveries have shown that deep inside their hives are special bees who act as living radiators to the other bees.

They keep the hive warm and maintain the temperature of the 'brood nest' where the pupae of young bees are developing into adults.

Different temperatures around the hive determine what type of bee they will become. Some will be the 'forager bees' who essentially collect supplies and bring them back to the nest. Others kept at a lower temperature will be the worker bees. They are always in the nest, feeding the larvae and doing the chores. The 'heater bees' beat the muscles controlling their wings and thus generate warmth.

A recent study shows the importance of all the different bees in the colony. There are the guard and nest building bees who do as their names suggest. There are brood caretaking bees and bees that take care of the queen bee. There are also the important forager bees. I suspect our visitor was one of them, although I feel he must have been a special nautical kind of bee. He must have been keen to give his sea legs a whirl and join us on old *Aeolus* for a sail.

What was he doing flying across the river anyway? Was he lost – or just caught up in the wind and travelling with it? After his rest he set of with confidence again. I will need to do some more research on these wonderful little creatures.

The River Stour and the Ganges Museum

Instead of sailing up the Orwell to Ipswich, we have sometimes taken the decision to explore the lovely River Stour and put in to Shotley Marina, which is in Harwich Harbour. It lies at the mouth of the river itself where it meets the Orwell.

This is a well managed Marina with 350 finger berths which have access to water and electricity, and 19 pontoons which make it so easy to go ashore or receive visitors.

In addition to this there is the 'Shipwreck' pub and restaurant, a chandlery, yacht broker and other useful facilities.

You enter the Marina via a lock (lat 51. 57' 43N, long 01 16'. 69E) which is managed 24 hours a day. The frequency to contact them is channel 80 or by phoning 01473 788982. You will be guided by marker posts approximately 50 feet apart which are both to port and starboard. There is also an Inogen leading light at starboard. This is an amazing invention which confirms whether you are in the correct channel by showing a black line in the centre of an orange screen. Any deviation from the correct route will change the vertical line to arrows which you should then follow.

Aeolus has a very shallow draught so she can arrive even at low tide. You will then be guided by the marina staff on Channel 80 or 37.

We love the peace of this marina and have found many useful items in the chandlery. Furthermore as we take our fold up bikes, it is so easy to go ashore with them on the pontoons.

In my log of 1984, I recorded that we stayed in the Stour for a night's anchorage and rowed ashore. We walked to the pub and had a game of darts. I wrote that the countryside was outstanding, covered with poppies and wild flowers. When we rowed back there were beautiful little phosphorus lights in the water.

We believed they were plankton. These also appeared when you flushed the water in the cabin. They were a truly magical sight.

We found out later that the painter John Constable was inspired to paint here. Thomas Gainsborough lived nearby at Sudbury. With all the locks and the barges which used to sail there surrounded by the beautiful countryside, it must have been an artist's paradise.

The Shotley Marina was once the sports area of the *HMS Ganges*. We walked along the river wall to see where it used to be situated. *HMS Ganges* was a training ship which moved from Falmouth to Shotley in 1899. In 1905, the training moved ashore where it continued until 1976 when it closed. The lovely building where young seamen used to train is now a listed building which can still be viewed from the road. The gem we discovered on the walk however, was the tiny, unique Ganges Museum. It is in the first building as you enter the Marina complex.

The collection there takes your breath away. Dedicated volunteers have amassed together a vast gathering of memorabilia including clocks, photos and documents so useful for further research. They have also acquired the figurehead from the original *HMS Ganges*. It is enormous and stands in pride of place in the museum.

A Lottery Grant from the Local Heritage Initiative enabled the purchase of computer equipment to be made along with the services of a professional cameraman to record and collate these Naval treasures for all time. This will be so useful to schools and other societies interested in the history of Navy training.

The museum is open Saturdays, Sundays, and Bank holidays between Easter and the end of October, 11am until 5pm and the last entrance is at 4.30pm. In December and January, visiting is by appointment only tel: 01787 228417. It is so worth a visit. We cannot wait to go again.

A Memory of the River Stour

Do you remember that week in June?
A boat trip sailing down the river
With friends and drinks and laughs?
Red gold setting sun and silver waves
And how at night small sea life
Dashed themselves against the oars
Causing ripples and rivulets of sharp
Fluorescent lights to flash through
The darkened depths of waves
Oh yes, we will remember that.

IPSWICH.

I have never got over the feeling of anticipation and excitement of sailing into Ipswich. You sail along the Orwell, past Felixstowe Port with its heavy industrial and loading areas, past huge ships, mainly from China with intriguing strange names, past pretty little Pin Mill, the Royal Harwich Yacht club, Woolverstone Marina, Stoke sailing club and many other picturesque sites. We next sail under the majestic Orwell Bridge which never fails to move me with the sight of her graceful lines and strength.

Once past the bridge, you see signs for the Port of Ipswich. You have to contact the Lock Control on VHF Ch68 for information on the lock times. There are lock signals at the entrance and as soon as they turn from red to green, you can enter according to the directions of the Lock Master. Life jackets must be worn however experienced you are due to the turbulence which can spring up out of nowhere.

I always find it interesting to go through a lock. There is so much going on and a land lubber like me has to keep alert. Sometimes people peer over and look at us as I try to look efficient while attempting to secure lines onto *Aeolus*.

Once through, you have the option of which marina you are heading for. There are two, Ipswich Haven Marina or Neptune Marina and both have excellent facilities. Again they can be contacted on Channel 68 and never seem to mind repeating their instructions if you do not hear correctly the first time.

These Marinas have the added thrill of being on Ipswich's doorstep. Ipswich is the county town of Suffolk and one of the oldest towns in England.

The Romans used it as a port and in the 7th century the Anglo Saxons made it into the largest port in the country. Looking at the harbour wall makes you wonder if parts of it are not from the original!

Once into the town you are spoilt for choice as to what to look at and where to go. We are fascinated by the Victorian swimming baths (still operational) which can be seen soon after leaving the marina. Then we trek to the transport museum which seems to be managed mostly by volunteers. This was so interesting and made us realise the painstaking work carried out in restoration of the many buses and vehicles there.

On my last visit to the museum I was impressed by an old 'Cumfi Folda' pushchair, the same as I had for my children. I asked permission and the very helpful assistant allowed me to push it round the museum. Mind you, it does make you feel a bit ancient when you see things you have used as an exhibit in a museum!

Avast ye land lubbers

Although our dear friends, Barbara and Alan, love to visit us when we are out on *Aeolus*, they would abhor the idea of joining us while we are sailing. Many places are ideal for a day visit and this is when they love to meet us and sit on board and enjoy an open air lunch prepared by Paul. After that we head off to explore the nearby town then return for a pub meal that lasts well into the evening. Ideal meeting places for this sort of rendezvous include Bradwell Marina, Walton on the Naze, Woodbridge and of course Ipswich.

Ipswich is an easy visit, within a day's drive from Leigh on Sea. The old town and harbour are a delight to explore with its Elizabethan Manor House, grounds and art treasures within easy walking distance of the marina. Of course there are plenty of cafes offering tasty choices and a variety of food nearby.

For longer visits Woodbridge Marina offers so many possibilities. Here our friends have stayed very happily at the lovely and very reasonable accommodation right near the Railway Station.

In Woodbridge you are spoilt for great choice of pub meals in the evening. However it is always best to book first as they are enormously popular.

At Walton on the Naze, in Titchmarsh, we have enjoyed a reasonable evening meal at the restaurant on the premises overlooking the Marina. This is always a treat. It is open to all and regularly busy. Barbara and Alan used to head to Clacton to stay at the Premier Travel Inn until they discovered some really reasonable little guest houses right on the front at Walton. How convenient is that?

Woodbridge

So, all in all our land lubber friends have the best of all worlds. Fresh sea air and the semblance of sailing whilst nicely moored up in a Marina, an open air lunch, excellent visiting agenda and a cosy bed on land for the night. What could be nicer?

Mascots

'I have yet to come across a boat that hasn't got some sort of mascot on board', is often quoted by sailing folk. In fact many boat owners boast about their mascots.

Yachting Monthly mentions one in 1999 named *Pepper Ted* who even had e-mails sent to him from abroad. Wooden parrots and a stuffed moose are also mentioned. Even one mascot who 'died' in a storm in Spain was given a wake by other mascots! So you see some sailors are softies at heart - especially Paul and I.

We have an unusual light grey Teddy Bear with blue eyes and a sailors cap which I found for sale on a ferry crossing the channel to France. 'Who's that for?' asked my mum. She could not believe it when I said 'Paul!'

Teddy has accompanied us on all our cruises in *Aeolus*; his cheery face brightening our dull days when the sun never seemed to shine and the rain came in droves. Once however, he suffered from a bad case of sea sickness and was upended from the small shelf on which he is kept.

So you can imagine the foreboding we felt when we discovered, on setting off on our holiday, that we had left him at home. I sent an urgent text to my daughter Sally. Could she pop him in a suitable container and give to our friends Barbara and Alan when they came to visit? 'Yes!' she replied, possibly thinking her parents had finally lost it! Meanwhile we felt lost without him. No cheerful grin in the mornings and no one to commiserate with about the rotten weather - just an empty space on the shelf. A nothingness!

While we were waiting for his arrival in a couple of weeks' time, Ipswich museum held the answer to our dilemma. A sale of small soft toys in aid of a charity was being held. Here we found little Hedgy and bought him for the princely sum of £1.50.

And the delightful thing was, when Ted finally turned up, he and Hedgy got on famously. And they have been good sailing companions ever since!

Aeolus after ready to go for new season

Essential for the shallows

Best mates Hedgy and Teddy

Captain Paul coming ashore at Pin Mill

Passing by Harwich. The lightship LV 18

Walton Tower a landmark for miles around

Red, Green and yellow marker buoys in the Thames estuary

79

Harbour Master Ramsholt Arms,

He guards this stretch of water
   on an ever present stand
Part of the scenery
   of sky and sea and land
Ensconced in an old boat
   but such a presence he
Directs with pointing finger
   and strong authority
Weathered brown his face
   and creased deep his eyes
The highest and the lowest boat
   comes under his surmise.
He will guard this harbour still
   until his dying day
And even then his presence will
   the physical outweigh
For at that time, when he is gone
   his memory will be there
Reflected in the swirling waves
   and in a seagull's stare.

Ramsholt and Prettyman's Point

If you fancy a quiet stop over before reaching the hurly burly of Woodbridge, there is no finer spot to be found than Ramsholt or Prettyman's Point.

Ramsholt, on the east bank of the River Deben, is a picturesque stretch of water, presided over by a helpful Harbour Master, George Collins, who took over from his father. Overlooking the harbour is a famous pub called the Ramsholt Arms. Years ago, it used to be a farmhouse. It still retains its lovely homely atmosphere. Here you can get a reasonably priced meal and, in fine weather, sit outside to enjoy the scenery. Prince Philip once stayed here in Room 1 - so it has a fine reputation.

We tend to row ashore at this beautiful place and walk along the sea wall to stretch our legs after a hectic sail. Sometimes we see fossil hunters on the beach collecting all kinds of prehistoric treasures such as coral. Ramsholt is one of the best places in Suffolk to find fossils. It is so relaxing. It is a great place to watch birds such as oyster catchers, avocets and brent geese.

Alternatively, following the sea wall you can cut inland along a well-used foot path to see the distinctive round tower of All Saint's Church.

Part of the church is Norman with a history going back hundreds of years. It fell into decay at one time due to a decreasing population but was restored in the 1850's.

Should we require a more peaceful time than even Ramsholt can offer, then we sail *Aeolus* a bit further along the River to anchor at a place called 'Prettyman's Point'. There are some most unusual names such as 'Loders Cut'. The 'Cut' is a man-made short cut built to help the marine trade, although I haven't as yet traced the origin of the name. It is such a natural spot and you can imagine it being in a film set for a desert island. Indeed, I think some filming has taken place here in the past.

You can still row ashore and enjoy the walk back to Ramsholt if you so wish, although it is a little more rugged. It is even possible to enjoy a pleasant swim in the clear water.

Prettyman's Point is my idea of heaven. Here *Aeolus* can drop her anchor and we know we are in for a peaceful evening with only the sound of the nightingales to disturb us. She will gently bump down and settle if we arrive at low water. But who cares, we will eventually float off again and resume our sailing once more.

Springer Spaniel at Ramsholt Arms

Little dog diving after stones
You're such a happy dog
At the edge of the water
Wagging your tail

Dipping and diving after stones
Thrown by your master
You'll never retrieve them
But chasing their ripples

To please him
Or is it yourself?
Pretending, to tease him
He knows and you know

The stones will sink
Without trace.

Aeolus crosses Harwich Harbour

However many times I have had it explained to me how we are going to cross this stretch of water, I always feel a little apprehensive. This is because of the enormous cargo ships and ferries which appear like dots on the horizon. They can move with enormous speed and in no time at all can appear almost beside us.

All leisure vehicles have to conform to the Safety of Life

Large container ships, for yachts it is best to keep out of their way!

at Sea Regulations (SOLAS). These are quite stringent and must be obeyed at all times. Reference to the Yachting guide to Harwich Harbour will show these Regulations and really they are mainly commonsense, especially when applied to this stretch of water.

The rules can look rather worrying until you realise that the massive container ships must keep between the red and green marked buoyage for their passage to and from the port of Felixstowe. There is a correct path for yachts to follow marked by a series of red dashes on the chart. This is not exclusive for yachts as motor and commercial boats can also use this route.

If you wish to proceed north to the River Deben from Walton on the Naze then you must cross as near to right angles as possible at the way points marked on the chart.

The chart recommends the wearing of life jackets to undertake this crossing and I always reach for mine in this area. Even though *Aeolus* is the steadiest of boats, it is good to take this precaution, because the wash from the big ships is so large.

Just to add to the nervous tension, remember that although you can see these huge ships, they cannot always see you. Therefore, once you have decided it is safe to cross, do so as quickly as possible.

Then you will soon see the Martello Towers on the Felixstowe Coast and know you have passed safely over the Shipping Lane. Phew! What a relief!

Harwich

Silent iron birds of prey
Wait to unload the freighter craft
Seals frolic in the sea below
And tiny ships sail timorously past.

The anxious sailor reads his chart
And prays no giants will bear down
Between the buoys both red and green
That mark the ongoing vessel's path.

Cranes lift freight that seem to hang
Still for a moment in mid air
East Goodwin light ship standing guard
Before they swing to land below.

Illusion at Pinmill

When I close my eyes
The silhouettes of boats remain
And shining rivers
Puff dark clouds
Upon the horizon
Seascape imprints
To fill the mind

With dreamless sleep.

Dowager London at Ipswich 2007
(Shoreham's RNLI Lifeboat)

At harbour now
A hulk of a ship
Retaining strength.

Formerly 'Rosa Wood'
Then 'Phyllis Lunn'
Now 'Dowager'.

Built 1932
Saved 143 lives
As a lifeboat.

3 trips from beaches of Dunkirk
Protecting men from shrapnel
With wheel house made from
Steel plate.   Dowager London

The Old Harbour Wall at Ipswich

Old harbour wall
With its ancient bricks
Fair covered with lichen
And mossy mould

Some bricks are new
In patchwork place
Some red, some yellow
And some slate grey

Mussels adhere to its slimy base
Rubber pipes spout over
Rust-capped outlets
In worm-worn wood

Yet stay - for here a spray
Of flowers, bright yellow
Delicate fronds are sprouting
From a crevice

The old harbour wall
With its history to tell
Still lives on
In spirit.

A Lithesome Visitor

When our granddaughter, Natalia aged 22, announced by text that she was coming to spend a few days with us on *Aeolus*, we were thrown into a bit of kerfuffle. We were at Ipswich and she was due to shortly arrive at the local railway station.

Although *Aeolus* was ideal for Paul and I and indeed on paper she can berth five people, in practice it would be very cramped.

Our granddaughter had been brought up in land locked Zimbabwe and although she was unused to life at sea she was a very daring young lady indeed. She had done a bungee jump over the Victoria Falls, parachuted in free fall from an aeroplane, camped rough in the wilds, rafted down African rivers and was a qualified scuba diver. We imagined she would consider it bit naff to be moored up with us 'oldies' whilst we pottered about on *Aeolus*.

My brother Derek came to the rescue. 'She can stay with me on my boat *Gratitude*', he said. We heaved a sigh of relief. Staying on *Aeolus* with her somewhat shabby cabins was one thing, but to be guest of honour on the immaculate, modern *Gratitude*, was another.

We met Natalia off the train at Ipswich and she gave a gasp of delight when she saw *Gratitude* looking as spruce as ever, waiting to greet her in the sunlight.

As soon as she got on board she took charge. Luckily she and Derek got on famously. We all sailed out of the Port of Ipswich with Natalia looking proud as a princess as she stood side by side with Derek on the deck.

We sailed up the Deben and dropped anchor at Waldringfield. As I prepared the evening meal, Paul made plans to pick Natalia up from *Gratitude* and Brian up from *Sapper*. But- '*Hi Nan!*' We looked over the side. There was Natalia, having dived off Derek's boat and swum over to join us, looking for all the world like a mermaid.

We had an enjoyable evening with Natalia showing us card tricks she had learned from the Southend Magic club. One was so clever - even she could not explain how it was done!

Next day she fancied having lunch at the Maybush pub but none of us old fogies wanted to. Undeterred she put her clothes in a plastic bag, then jumped overboard, swimming with them held in one hand over her head.

When she reached the shore, she washed off her muddy legs at the stand pipe then dried herself off to get dressed and went for her meal.

Of course, all this was a treat for Derek, Paul and Brian. Sometimes their eyes seemed to come out on stops!

Such a lithesome young miss in her bikini most of the time, looking like a young model. I just felt amazed at her daring!

When we arrived at Woodbridge, it was time for her to pack up her rucksack and set off once more on her adventures. I have to say we missed her company. It all seemed a bit tame after she left!

My Brother Derek

My brother Derek has been so helpful to Paul and I and is such a sailing character. I feel he needs an article to himself.

He first owned the lovely little 22 foot wooden maple leaf yacht, *Golden Harvest*. It was everything a traditional sailor could wish for, but hard work to maintain.

In 1985, he decided to look for a fibreglass boat. He found a 26 foot Westerley Griffin by the name of *Gratitude* at Chichester. He was so impressed with the boat, he decided to sail her home to Leigh-on-Sea that same day.

Derek was undecided whether he liked the name *Gratitude* for his boat and considered changing it but I persuaded him that it was an excellent one.

After all, to be in good health and out at sea, capturing the elements of wind and tide, surely there is every reason to feel real gratitude.

Derek is a joker. Our trips have benefitted not only from his guidance but also his sense of fun. For example, he has a box of different hats on board. It really does look funny to see him and his crew when they wear them.

Hats to the fore Derek and Natalia

Imagine the captain in a bowler hat and you will see what I mean. He is an early riser and loves to be the first away in the morning. Sometimes a potato will land on deck with a message scratched on it to get us sleepy heads going.

He is very competent and holds an Off Shore Yachtmaster's qualification. He is always ready to help or advise novice sailors. He helps to organize the combined clubs series involving the handicaps of boats wishing to race locally. His boat is immaculate and he can be quite fussy. We all bear this in mind when we come aboard. Nicknamed 'Captain Birdseye', I believe he lives up to it. His friend, Brian Little, proud owner of *Sapper*, a 26 foot Westerly Centaur, has also joined us on recent voyages. We are lucky to have such stalwart sailing companions.

VILLANELLE sailing alongside Waldringfield

To go with the flow of the wind and tide
At one with nature the boat and the sea
I see the sails billowing open wide

Let me find respite from the storm and hide
A tiny harbour will do fine for me
To go with the flow of the wind and tide

There's no place for boasting or undue pride
With the gulls and sky in true harmony
I see the sails billowing open wide

With new ways left for those tested and tried
I use my good knowledge so skilfully
To go with the flow of the wind and tide

The gold evening light will act as my guide
Red buoy to port and the starboard to lee
I see the sails billowing open wide

Across the still waves the boat seems to glide
Alone with my craft I arrive safely
To go with the flow of the wind and tide
I see the sails billowing open wide.

The Entrance to the River Deben

Sailing into the River Deben can be a hazardous experience due to the shifting sand banks at its entrance. It is essential to have the latest information and chart showing the position of these as they do change every year. It will also show the position of the West Knoll Red and Mid Knoll Green buoys to guide you through. We never attempt this fast flowing entrance if there is a strong northerly wind blowing, as it would stir the waves up too much and would prove too dangerous a passage for a small sailing boat like *Aeolus*.

We try to arrive on the last of the outgoing tide from Harwich, then wait around until sufficient water builds up with the incoming tide so that if we should become stuck on going in, we will soon be able to float off again. As *Aeolus* draws less than the rest of our small flotilla at only two and a half feet, we usually lead the way in.

Although the entrance is a tricky one with all of us on our mettle, it is so worthwhile to negotiate in order to pass through and enter this beautiful River.

Fog on the River Deben

It all looks different in the fog
Ships like spectres loom
And trees are marauding monsters
Silent on the shore.

All is damp
And the air heavy
Slowly slowly it begins to lift
And turns into soft mist.

Shapes emerge into their true selves
Sun begins to play on masts
People and boats become real
No longer occupy the world of ghosts.

Woodbridge.

After sailing along the River Deben, a welcome stop is the Tidemill Yacht Marina at Woodbridge. Paul and I have been visiting it for years and still feel an excited surge of anticipation as we pick up a buoy and wait at the entrance to the marina. It has recently improved its facilities and after several days sailing, the thought of a hot shower is very appealing.

You have to make sure that the depth of water over the bar at the entrance to the marina is sufficient to allow your boat to pass over it. The instructions are relatively easy and can be determined beforehand by consulting a tide table. However, it is essential to know what your boat's draught is. It is also necessary to take into account the weight of passengers, fuel and water etc.

Aeolus' draught is only two and a half feet which very useful for exploring shallow waters. Going into the marina you will also see a tide gauge at the entrance. This is ultimately the instruction to make note of.

Once moored up it often difficult to choose what to do. There is so much on offer. Sometimes we take our fold-up bikes and further explore the coast line. Alternatively you can wander round Woodbridge town itself and take in the fascinating views of barges and boats. Woodbridge has superb restaurants, pubs, ice-cream parlours, a theatre combined with a cinema - in fact you are really are spoilt for choice. Charity shop fans will find many precious bargains, with one dedicated solely to books. Are we in heaven I ask myself?

One shop we head for straight away is the bakery on the left hand side of the High Street. We recommend to get there early though, because they are soon sold out!

The most delicious bread you have ever tasted is there with wonderful names like 'King Ranulf's', bread made with ingredients such as honey and other delicious items. My mouth waters at the thought of it.

Budgen's Supermarket is just behind the main street for a good stock up of provisions including a bag of ice to keep them cool if it is hot. When we go there, I always seem to see a little dog waiting outside tied up with his leash. Can't be the same one surely!

Dog Waiting at Budgen's

Little dog waits out in the rain
Bedraggled and shivering what would he say
If he could talk?
'Take me for a walk?'
No -

'My master has gone away
Must I wait here all day?'
His pleading eyes I cannot stand -
At last! His master is at hand.

Snoring

At first it came like a distant roar
Softly at first then more and more
A full throated snarl through an open jaw
Yes this was it – the dreaded snore!

Historical Woodbridge.

If you are interested in history and art, then again Woodbridge is a superb place to visit.

First there is the Tidemill. There was a tide mill on this spot in the 12th century operated by the Augustinian Canons. It is fascinating to look at this point in the river and think that such a power from water had been harnessed so long ago. The mill passed to King Henry VIII in 1536. After the dissolution in 1564, Queen Elizabeth I granted it to Thomas Seckford (a prominent Woodbridge citizen).

The present building dates from 1793 and it was restored and opened to the public in 1975. In 2004 it received a lottery grant. The mill, which dominates the view of the River Deben, is now considered to be a star attraction for visitors. It is open every day in the summer from 11am to 5pm.

A short walk away from the mill is the Woodbridge Art Club founded in 1968. This is a must for me to explore when it is open because it contains a wealth of local art, lace and pottery for sale, some at reasonable prices.

You cannot walk very far in Woodbridge without coming across evidence of the 16th century benefactor, Sir Thomas Seckford mentioned above. He was a lawyer, politician and friend of influential William Cecil, later Lord Burghley.

He was acutely aware of the poverty of the elderly and a very generous and far seeing man. Bequests he made in those times are still in evidence today and still support the less fortunate. He had almshouses built for 13 poor men and formed the Seckford Foundation to support the hospital, school and library. The almshouse buildings still survive there today as a monument to his generosity. As you walk along Seckford street, it is amazing to think of this great man, still remembered and valued today.

In the tiny museum in the High Street there is a great deal more information about Seckford and his good works. It is open Thursday to Sunday between 10am and 4pm.

There is also information about another famous citizen of this area, Edward Fitzgerald, who translated Omar Khayam and lived in nearby Melton from 1809 to 1883. A blue plaque can be seen on the wall of his house in Pytches Road, placed there by the Woodbridge Society.

Fitzgerald kept his boat *Scandal* on the river Deben and brought many literary people to the town including Carlyle and Tennyson. They stayed at the Bull Hotel, Woodbridge, which, as then, still overlooks the market square.

Paul and I made a pilgrimage to see Fitzgerald's grave in St Michael and All Angels graveyard at Boulge which is three miles from Woodbridge. Here Fitzgerald is buried under a rose tree which was grown from hips taken from Omar Khayyam's grave at Nishapur. How poignant is that!

Charity Shop at Woodbridge

All these hats
Worn once with
pride
At weddings
Just to bless the
bride

To see and
be seen in
Now inside
Glass case for
Sale at knock down
prices

Second hand.

Mud and a stormy day at Woodbridge

Mud the colour of curdled cream
Creeps around the bottoms
Of old restored barges

The tide laps to shore
Froth laden with scum
Heralded by clink of ships' battens and stays

As they chink and tink against stalwart masts
But the wayward gulls are quiet today
As if they foretell the oncoming storm.

Barge Arrayed with Flowers(Woodbridge)

Old barge arrayed with flowers
Your cargo days are over
Now hours of leisure come your way.

Curtains at portholes
Barbecue aft deck
Set with table and garden chairs

New owners delighting in comfort
Like you their days
Now spent at ease.

Mauve petunias and geraniums stand
In earthenware pots on cabin roof
All petals dancing in the fine sea breeze.

Boatyards

With a few hours to while away until the next sail, (for me) there can be no more interesting place to browse in than a boatyard. When at Woodbridge, one of our favourite places to look round is Andy Seedhouse's boatyard. All types of boats are up for sale or stored there.

As I look round I start thinking about the people who have sailed these boats, either recently or in the past. Some boats seem to be crying out to be back in the water again. They appear to be thoroughly fed up with resting on their haunches and waiting for a prospective buyer.

For under £300 a small 'mirror' type sailing dinghy can be bought. These are so useful to learn how to sail on and very nostalgic for Paul and I to see as we owned a similar model for four years prior to owning *Aeolus*. They have a lifting centreboard keel. They are an ideal boat to learn all the rudiments of sailing. The 'mirror' can also take a two HP engine which is useful if the wind should drop.

A visit to Andy's website shows all the various designs and models they have to offer. For me though, when I look round, I love to see the more unusual homemade projects. I believe that the fun in some of them was in their making rather than sailing them.

How exciting it must be to design and plan a boat then to work away building and equipping her with your schemes in mind. It might take years to do but who cares? The project may one day be finalised but that won't stop you getting lost in the seas of your imagination. Even if that day never comes, at least you will have some fun thinking of where your burgeoning project might take you while you continue working away and dream on.

Andy Seedhouse's Boatyard

Want a dinghy?
Want a boat?
Want to spend some time afloat?
Look no further
Here you'll find
A boat to suit you
Just your kind.

Fancy a trip? Aladdin's cave?
Want to buy but also save?
Here you'll find a little gem
Sparkling like a diadem.
First rub down and make amends
Enlist the help of trusted friends
Andy Seedhouse's the place to be

Just at Woodbridge by the sea.

A Walk along the Sea Wall to Sutton Hoo

However, the most famous historical spot on our voyage is Sutton Hoo. Turning right after leaving Woodbridge Yacht Marina and walking a short distance along the road past Woodbridge Art premises there is a small entrance to a public footpath leading along the sea wall to Sutton Hoo.

This walk is an annual treat for Paul and I. In my opinion no other historical site can evoke so much anticipation as this one. As we approach we see many wrecks, including some from the last world war, disintegrating or gently rotting away in the river. Each provokes different thoughts of their origins and their final downfall.

Thoughts of the history of the Deben come into mind as it has been the scene of both Viking and Anglo-Saxon incursions. Of course the river has greatly changed in the last 1000 years but anyone with imagination can picture some of these events.

Sutton Hoo itself is a National Trust site now but as we have been visiting it for 24 years, Paul and I have known it for a long time. Of course the main attraction is the undisturbed ship burial site and the adjacent cemetery mounds dating from the 6th or 7th century.

As you enter the site, with its newish impressive museum building, you cannot help but feel pride in all the effort that has gone into showing this site to its full advantage. A small fee entitles you to have the services of an excellent guide who will show you round the area – a must, if you are to enjoy it to the full.

As you walk to the site proper, you will see Sutton Hoo House, where Mrs Edith Pretty in 1938, with her interest in spiritualism, felt she wanted to engage Mr Basil Brown in excavating the burial mounds. Basil Brown was a local archaeologist with knowledge of Suffolk soil.

He was passionate about his work and an excellent choice even though, when the site became famous, he was overruled by pompous big wigs from the British Museum.

We go there every year and return to *Aeolus* with a sense of fulfilment that we have viewed again some of the wonderful treasures on show. We now plan to visit the British Museum where even more of the Sutton Hoo treasures are displayed.

Brother Derek models a Saxon Helmet at Sutton Hoo

The Cutting Room Floor

The cloth lies languid on the cutting room floor
Waiting for the patternmaker's chalk
And the sharp edge of the cutter's shears.

Machinists play their measured grind
While disturbed dust trickles down in sunlight
From the raftered roof of the warehouse.

Now a small motif is added
And the sails declared finished.
Soon they'll be hoisted up on the mast.

The sails will shake off their lethargy
Filling and blossoming out in the wind
Taking the boat with them;

They will become part of the horizon
Part of the clouds, part of the sky
Alive, now they've left the cutting room floor.

Neuralgia at Sea

Neuralgia is excruciatingly painful when you are at sea. You cannot escape the elements and even codeine does not seem to touch it.

I had severe neuralgia one very hot afternoon in June when we were approaching Woodbridge Harbour. One of my 'remedies' for neuralgia to ease the pain, regardless of the temperature, is to lay my head on a warm hot water bottle and I would not wittingly put to sea without one. But on this occasion I had left mine at home.

The pain grew more intense as we arrived in the marina. Once we had secured *Aeolus* on a mooring, Paul and I hurried along to Boots the Chemist to buy a new hot water bottle.

'Sorry just closing,' an assistant informed us. 'In any case, we have none in stock this time of year. Try over the road at Lloyds.' We did this and the assistant there told us she would look in their stock room. To my relief, she came back with one. It was a lovely pink fleece covered hot water bottle. We paid for it and left the shop.

Well, that definitely was the cure. As soon as we stepped out into the street with my hot water bottle – the pain completely vanished! Psychological or what? O.K. it is not macho, but I have known hardy men wishing they had one, even if they would not admit it, especially after a hard, wet, cold day's sailing.

The only cup that we gained with *Aeolus* was won on such a day. Not a first prize you may note, but one with 'For Perseverance' written on it.

We were in a friendly race which we should have had more sense than to enter as *Aeolus* only covers, at top speed, four nautical miles per hour and six or seven on an exceptional day. It was nightfall as we limped into Pyefleet Creek which was the finishing point. All the other boats were moored up and out of kindness had lit their lanterns to guide us in. It was freezing and we were perished.

The only way I could get warm was to stand in a bowl of hot water, eat a bowl of hot rice pudding and drink a goodly shot of hot water and whiskey before getting into my sleeping bag with the aforesaid hot water bottle.

The funny thing was that in the morning I woke up bright as a button with no sign whatsoever of the dreaded neuralgia. The body is a strange thing and I reckon we deserved that cup. 'Perseverance' really does sum up sailing at times!

Neuralgia at Sea

Through wind and rain
Comes throbbing pain
Migraine or tooth
Or vein
Neuralgic bane.

Knock back codeine
What's the use?
Pain won't declare
A needed truce.

Ah bliss of numbed nerves
All calm again.

Relief from Pain

When pain lifts
The relief is greater
Than any calm
After storm.

The soul gives thanks
The spirit lifts up
The body relaxes
Back to the norm

Who does what on Aeolus

Like a lot of women on board a boat, I suppose I could be called 'cack-handed'. Oh I know there are some very competent female souls out there who can stride up to the mast and haul up the sails, or step smartly for'ard holding the boat hook to neatly pick up a mooring buoy but unfortunately I am not one of these. No – when given a rope to throw to someone on shore, it usually lands in the water and I have to try again. Told to place a rope round the stanchion and back to the cleat, mine is always round the wrong way and I have to pass it through again.

Mind you- I am not alone. I once saw a charming lady pumping out the bilge whilst chatting to a friend but holding the end of the pump so that it fed the water back into the bilge again. At least I have never done that!

Some men get very angry with their wives when they do not carry out instructions to the 'T' and are not slow to release a string of diatribe at them, not in a quiet way either. I don't think I could stand that!

My role is more of companionship and support. (Paul's words, not mine.) After all, someone has to write the poetry and appreciate the flow of nature. Paul does all the shopping, cooking and washing up on board and he says that I deserve a true break - as I do all the cooking, shopping and washing the rest of the year. It's no wonder I enjoy sailing so much!

In case you are wondering just what I do, I keep the cabin tidy and occasionally set to and polish the wood work. My brother says *Aeolus* is the only boat he knows which smells of furniture polish. I also operate the ship's radio and hold an official operator's licence. This does seem to qualify my existence as 'crew'.

Things I won't miss when leaving the Boat

Washing up in 2 inches of water
Turning the gas bottle on and off
Flushing the toilet with a small pump action
Trying to keep the food cold
Sniffing food to see if it is off
Just missing the weather forecast.

Things I will miss when leaving the Boat

Looking out onto a calm sea
The cry of sea birds
The sky at sun set
The sky at sun rise
The companionship of other sailors
The gentle rocking before sleep.

A Clothes Peg Overboard

A clothes peg fell overboard today
It dropped with a plop
Then floated away.

I followed it as far as the
eye could see
A miniature destroyer
Of enemy.

Previously holding a shirt
and a vest
Now called to duty
At Nature's behest.

Skirting the sea-weed
And riding the waves
Clothes pegs will never
succumb to be slaves.

Goodbye valiant clothes peg
I've now found another
I hope it will hold fast:-
Not slip - like its brother.

Dinner Parties on Board Aeolus

You may think it is a bit incongruous to hold a dinner party on board a sailing boat. Indeed, on the wrong evening it can prove a bit rocky.

Aeolus has only a small grill and two gas burners so cooking is pretty basic. The rule is - keep it simple but serve as immaculately as possible. This will help it to be a really memorable occasion.

A tablecloth effect can be achieved by placing a brand new nautical tea towel on the small chart table. Nice place mats and sparkling wine glasses will show your guests that you have made a good effort. We bought some fish knives and forks from a charity shop in Aldeburgh and these make it a bit special if you are having fish.

One successful dinner party we gave on board *Aeolus* was really easy and was made up as follows:-

One ready cooked crab per person. (Woodbridge has a small fish stall near the bus station which specialises in these.) A bowl of appetizing salad, a bowl of cooked potatoes and some new crusty French bread – my mouth melts at the memory.

For the second course try a sherry trifle. This was made quite easily beforehand using a small stale sponge, spread with jam, covering it in sherry and adding fruit salad, ready made custard and cream. Fortunately I had remembered to pack a whisk. Decorated with small flaked toasted almonds it was delicious!

We finished up with cheese and biscuits which made the meal a real success.

More Ambitious Cooking on Board

Paul experimented this year and found that fish can be cooked on board, but of course the smells had to be strictly monitored to prevent them infiltrating the whole of the boat. He achieved this by wrapping the fish in tin foil and grilling until it is cooked. The smells were contained and now it is such a delight to be able to buy fresh fish from the fishermen on shore at Aldeburgh then present it to guests, or enjoy it ourselves, as a special treat.

Another easy meal to prepare is a ready cooked chicken or some cold pressed beef bought from a good supermarket. Again it should be served with some salad and potatoes as before. Be sure a merry evening will ensue.

Should the weather be freezing cold (as some summer evenings can be) a complete meal cooked in one large saucepan can be the answer. Meat such as nuggets of pork or small pieces of chicken cooked in a sauce of tomatoes, mushrooms and onions and simmered with other complimentary vegetables will be entirely acceptable. But remember to try to keep the cooking smells down as much as possible. Open all vents and if you have a small fan turn it on full blast.

A good standby for guests is wholemeal spaghetti served with a sauce of onions, mushrooms, tomatoes and vegetables. This is handy if you are not too sure how many will turn up. Any left over can be reheated next day. With meals such as these, you cannot beat the ready made sweet from the supermarket. After all you – the cook – are on holiday as well. Naturally the meal will be complemented by a good bottle of wine or two (my favourite is Rosé) and it will be the perfect meal.

Bon Appetite!!

The Bell at Orford Haven Buoy

I wanted to hear the sound of the bell
But whether I heard it I could not tell
For it mingled with sighs and the sound of the sea
The shifting of shingle and sand by degree.

But there in my innermost ear insisted
The sound of that Orford bell still persisted
A lone and sonorous note out at sea
Still warning the sailors of danger's decree.

I can't hear it now but its memory remains
Forever its watch o'er the seas' grim domains.

Aeolus at Orford

Church and Castle viewed in one glance
Sandbanks each side measured by gulls
Swans glide against the tide
Aeolus sails furled follows the flow.

The River Ore

Coming into the River Ore offers the yachtsman the unique experience of being able to view both a church and a castle in one glance. Sometimes, if the sea is calm you can just glide in with a convoy of sedate swans.

Orford Castle was built by Henry II in the 1160's to counterbalance the power of East Anglian barons and also to guard the coast against attack from foreign mercenaries. Its polygonal tower keep was built as an 18 sided drum with three square turrets. It is a must to visit when you go ashore. The castle is owned by English Heritage and the entrance fee is very reasonable. An excellent audio guide takes you back to historic times so you do not miss anything. The views from the top are outstanding. Furthermore the castle's original building accounts are still intact and can be inspected. These make interesting reading!

There are also accounts of the 'Merman' of Orford who was washed up in 1207. This is a fascinating tale for all those who like a mixture of truth and legend. It is about a strange man who appeared to live in the sea. He was captured and refused to speak despite being hung upside down by the feet!

Orford Church is also worth a visit. It was built around the same time as the castle and later rebuilt in the 14th century. There was another major restoration carried out in the 1890's when the south west buttress gave way. However the original font is still in place.

Benjamin Britten, who lived at Aldeburgh, loved this church. The architecture is believed to have been the inspiration in some of his works. Orford is a good place to stock up on provisions. There is a small village shop selling almost everything and a quality butchers' just round the corner to it, whose homemade pies, venison sausages and first class beef steaks make the visit well worth while.

There is also a smokery with its lovely appetizing smells to guide you and tempt you into making a purchase. Next to the smokery there is a small building where you can buy a magazine or newspaper by placing your money in the collecting box.

Not many places today boast such a belief in honesty!

Orford Castle

River Ore

Lobster pots and
Martello tower
Announce the entrance
Of River Ore.

The Haven Buoy
Takes you in
And two more Martellos
Like sentries stand.

Wartime defence
In years gone by
Still stand guard
But now at peace.

The Orford lighthouse
red and white
Will flash her beams
Throughout the night.

The River Butley

Instead of sailing directly down the River Ore to Orford, we sometimes branch off along its tributary, the River Butley. Once called Butley Creek it flowed to Butley Mill, operational from the 1530's until it silted up in 1948.

There are remains of an iron-age pottery near Butley and a study of place names nearby, such as Iken and Eyke, suggest that the local tribe in Roman times were the Iceni. Now there is just the ambience of ancient history as you view the reed banks and flat marshes on either side of the river.

There is a charted anchorage at the mouth of the Butley or you can sail further down to anchor near the old red brick quay wall with a ruined building on the port side. This is where the barges once tied up to collect their cargo of hay bound for London. You can still climb up here and see the amazing stillness of the river as it winds though the Suffolk countryside.

You can also tie up the tender on the other side of the river and take a pleasant walk into Orford itself. Be careful though! We were returning from this walk one day carrying a delicious warm mince and onion pie that we had bought from the local butcher when we saw an amazing sight on the opposite bank.

There sat *Aeolus,* for all the world looking as if she had jumped high and dry out of the water, surrounded by sloping squelchy mud. There was no reaching her so we had to settle down for a few hours waiting for the tide to turn sufficiently for us to row out.

Luckily we had that lovely mince pie to eat or we too would have been high and dry. We each plugged an ear in to Paul's small radio and whiled away a few hours until the tide came in again. We finally climbed on board very exhausted and fell into our bunk beds. Even so everything was still on the slant until the tide was fully up. It was certainly a novel experience.

The Mysterious Orford Ness

After years of sailing round to Orford along the River Ore we thought we had seen most of what this beautiful countryside had to offer - 'The Mysterious Orford Ness!' Well, we all like a bit of mystery don't we?

At Orfordness, small almost Egyptian or pagoda like structures can be seen along the coast. We must have passed them by many times but never registered what we were looking at. They are military buildings and have been there since the First World War.

But wait a minute, all this is hush hush isn't it? Well it used to be. The buildings were used until the end of the Cold War. All the time they were continually adapted as the military tested different materials.

However, now, courtesy of The National Trust, visitors are allowed to visit for as long as they like and take photographs provided they keep to specified routes. How exciting is that!

National Trust wardens will lead the tours and give tips on how to take some good photos. The Orford Ness site was first bought by the Department of War in 1913. A prominent building to be seen is the Orford Ness Rotating Wireless Beacon, also known as the 'Black Beacon' on account of its colour. It was built in 1928 and designed as an early radio navigation system whereby ships or aircraft with conventional radio receivers could measure their angle to the station.

The romantic looking little pagoda type buildings, in contrast to their looks, were built for research into explosive design. Any gasses let off by an accidental explosion would be vented and dissipated in a contained way with the roof designed set to collapse and seal the contents in with concrete.

However the tours themselves are quite expensive:-
£60.00 for members of the public or £50.00 for members
of the National Trust. (A useful phone number for further
information is 01394 450900).

For the time being we will content ourselves with a quick
peek as *Aeolus* sails majestically by. Still it is nice to know
what's going on regarding activities in this stretch of the
Ore.

The Mysterious Black Beacon at Orfordness

Boat in the Sunset

Fair sails the fairy boat out to sea
As light as thistledown fair sails she.
Oh skim the waters of the tide
The trail you leave is the trail of a bride.
Into the sunset's gold you go
Carrying your cargo safe below,
Of gossamer silk and fairy wine
Of gold and jewels and all of it mine.

Aldeburgh

Aldeburgh is such a special place to sail to. The River Ore needs to be negotiated with care as it can be deceptively shallow and even experienced sailors have gone aground in these waters.

Aldeburgh means 'old fort'. Coming into the harbour gives you a sense of great history and tradition. Indeed at one time Aldeburgh was famous for ship building. Francis Drake's Golden Hind was built here.

Although the Yacht Club is very welcoming in that you can make use of their facilities, they only seem to have a few visitors' moorings. You can however pick up one from Upson's Boatyard for £5.00 per night.

The tide can be very fast here and you have to pick your moment when to row ashore. Once the pull of the tide was so strong, we had to get a lift from the club boat on our return as it was impossible to row against it.

The walk along the front to the town is very invigorating. There is much to see with the pretty little cottages along the side of the road. You can also see a building which on first sight looks like a folly but on closer inspection reveals that it is a disused windmill, built in 1824 and converted into a four storey house in 1902. It is known as fort green mill. The inscription over the door is in Danish and translated means 'The Lord shall preserve thy going out and thy coming in'. It is now used as a holiday home.

At the time of writing Aldeburgh beach has a 'blue flag'. It is a shingle beach and became a resort in Victorian days. You can see much of the architecture is from these times. As you progress along the beach you can see the 400 year old Moot House with its fine Tudor details. The council still meets there – how proud they must feel at continuing such an ancient tradition.

Reflection at Aldeburgh

The bird and his reflection
Stands by the shore
But which is which
He is not sure.

Although he feels a certain lust
There's much about it he doesn't trust
The turn of his head so like his own
Narcisstic stare but he's all alone.

He plunges his beak into the sea
And picks up food with a feeling of glee
The ripples now mask his rival's face
And suddenly everything falls into place.

Other Attractions at Aldeburgh

There are many eating places and pubs to catch your eye. In our pre-cholesterol days, we would head for one of the fish and chips shops along the High Street, owned by the Cooney family and reputed to be the best in the U.K. Nowadays we just indulge ourselves in a satisfying sniff as we walk by and head off to buy some freshly caught fish which we can cook ourselves.

Something not to be missed is the enormous lifeboat in its own building. It fills me with awe as I look round reading the story boards of the lives they have saved. The little lifeboat shop next door is also a must to stock up on writing cards illustrated with sea scenes. Once purchased, they will last me for the winter.

A sight along the beach which has not received universal approval is *The Scallop*, a sculpture dedicated to the memory of Benjamin Britten.

The work was made in stainless steel by artist Maggi Hambling, a Suffolk painter and sculptor, and is one of the most famous sculptures in England. It was unveiled on the beach in 2003 and cost £75,000.

As its name suggests it is two large shell like structures. *The Scallop* seems to have won over the objections raised by locals when it was first put up. Although it suffers from periodic vandalism, its image appears on postcards and mugs throughout the town. For us it is a pleasure to sit in *The Scallop* and eat sandwiches.

Talking of Benjamin Britten, he of course is such a famous son of Aldeburgh. He lived with his partner Peter Pears in Crag House from 1947 to 1957. Later they moved to Red House, Golf Lane, Aldeburgh and lived there until their respective deaths in 1976 and 1986. Red House has recently been awarded a large grant from the Lottery Fund and has greatly improved its facilities.

From June 2013 there will be a free exhibition open all the year round. If you wish to visit the House itself, it will be open from June 2013 until the end of September. It will be essential to book for this and at the time of writing the entrance fee has yet to be decided. Further details can be obtained from The Britten Pears foundation on 01728 451700 or by looking at www.brittenpears.org or e-mail at reveal@britten.pears.org. We visited the Library adjoining the Red House and found such a poignant atmosphere there. We felt as though these two gifted men would presently bound into the room with their enthusiasm and vivacity.

Further useful information on the happenings in Aldburgh can be obtained from the information office tel (01728 453637) at their new address of 48, High Street Aldeburgh, open every day except Sunday from 10 am to 3 pm.

Approaching Snape

I always took the name 'Snape' to mean a snake-like river. However the name originates from the Anglo Saxon words Snape, Snapes or Snapys, meaning bog or marsh. Snape was a straggling group of cottages or small farms beside a marshy river bed and lanes leading inland. It certainly has a rich history which can be traced over 2,000 years with both Roman and Norman connections.

If you sail, you need to approach Snape from the River Alde on a rising tide, approximately half flood, so that if you should land on a mud bank you will be able to float off again and resume your journey. On your return you should leave an hour before high water. After leaving Slaughden Quay at Aldeburgh, you proceed along the river Alde in a westerly direction following the beacons to port and starboard.

You then sail past Iken Church towards the Iken cliffs where a safe anchorage can be made. At night an anchor light is advisable in case of passing boats. Also the anchor should be buoyed because of submerged old mooring chains. We decided to anchor *Aeolus* there for the night with *Gratitude* nearby, so that preparations could be made for us to sail to Snape the next day.

During the night, however, despite our night lights all aglow, there was panic aboard both vessels when a further boat anchored nearby, to our horror, became very close as they had not correctly estimated their length of anchor chain. We all rushed on board in our pyjamas carrying torches and it is surprising how near a boat can be without actually touching. Oh yes, it does not do to be complacent even in the quietest of rivers.

If you wish to sail to Snape and back again in one day, you must pay special attention to the tides. Care must also be taken as to whether your boat can negotiate these somewhat shallow waters. Again we are lucky here because *Aeolus* draws less than two metres.

It is a difficult route along this tortuous twisting part of the river because you have to concentrate on keeping the markers on the right side of the boat. When we sailed there, these were simply red capped twigs to the left and green capped twigs to the right going in and vice versa going out.

Both *Aeolus* and *Gratitude* got stuck on the banks at different times. *Aeolus* got off by reversing her engine so that was relatively simple. Derek, drawing slightly more, had to wait for the tide to float him off.

Of course, if you are a Benjamin Britten enthusiast, you can sail right up to the harbour wall, change into appropriate clothing and hop off to attend a Benjamin Britten Festival.

The famous Snape Maltings concert hall was built in 1967 and in June each year is host to the Aldeburgh Festival, started in 1948 by Benjamin Britten and Peter Pears. Even if you are not a music lover there is plenty to see at the Maltings. There are art and craft shops, country wear and natural food shops.

We tied *Aeolus* next to *Gratitude*, which Derek had tied to the harbour wall. People watched us admiringly as there was not much else going on that day. That seemed to make the rigours of the night all worthwhile! It is a beautiful part of the river and well worth a visit.

Visitors Books

We have a visitor's book on board *Aeolus* but no one has written in it yet. We always forget to get it out. My brother Derek, on *Gratitude*, has kept one for years.

He sails on his own or with friends. Some of their comments suggest some of the beery times they have had while on board. I know one of his friends actually fell overboard. Luckily Derek was able to fish him out again.

I decided to add my own little verses to his visitor's book to 'higher the tone' and also to cause him some embarrassment if his friends should read it. After all, I am 'Big Sis', or 'Mastermind'.

He calls me 'Mastermind' on account of what happened years ago when he and his school friends formed what they thought of as a secret society with coded messages left in a hole in our fence. I discovered these messages one day, decoded their contents and left bogus replies in their place. Sometimes I signed off as 'Mastermind'. He never found out it was me until years later.

Derek is quite a sailing character and it is mainly due to his patience and expertise that we have managed to gain confidence in navigating the rivers. It is also a great comfort to have him with his lovely boat, *Gratitude*, already tied up and waiting for us at a mooring.

Aeolus has a nice little diesel engine and is fine at going forward, but she has a mind of her own when reversing. This can be a drawback, especially when coming out of a marina on a blowy day. The horrified look of other owners as we almost ricochet out of the marina, with me on the front ready to fend off with my foot, is not one I relish.

Although we have been sailing for many years we still regard ourselves as 'green'. I remember the time when we both jumped out onto the small harbour wall at Rowhedge on the River Colne, each expecting the other one to have hold of the rope, then discovering that neither of us had it.

The sight of *Aeolus* majestically sailing off with no one onboard is one that I will remember for a very long time. Luckily Paul is quite an expert in leaping back onto her!

We do not get many visitors on *Aeolus*. Sometimes I wonder why!!

Writing in *Gratitude's* Visitors Book.

11.06.2001

I thought I saw a ship
Sailing 'neath the stars
With silver on her mast
And gold upon her spars.

18.05.2005

I thought I saw the captain
A reaching out for me
And so I stepped aboard
To sail that starry sea.

22.06.2007

The waves were tipped with moonshine
And the captain's face was bold
I stood and watched a magic world
Before my eyes unfold.

Sirens

I sometimes hear the sirens sing
When I'm out at sea
Their voices have a plaintive ring
Or so it seems to me

They sing of silver and of gold
And all life's mystery
Of sailors simple, sailors bold
All lost to history

But I must keep my course held tight
Ignore their winsome cries
Lest I with them should seek respite
From heavy storm-filled skies.

Nautical Terms

It is fun to use a few of these terms whilst sailing or indeed at any time you feel like a bit of nautical flavour in your speech.

Above board	All as you see it on deck.
All at sea	Feeling unbalanced and disorientated.
All hands on deck	Everyone help!
Any port in a storm	Safety is the first issue.
At a loose end	Nothing to do.
Batten down the hatches	(One of my favourites.) Secure everything well.
Bilge	Talking rubbish. Like waste water in the bilge.
Broad in the beam	Applies to boats as well as large women.
Calm before the storm	Obvious meaning.
Clear the decks	Make a clean sweep of everything.
Cut and run	Cut off anchor chain in a sticky situation.
Don't rock the boat	Keep your thoughts to yourself to avoid a row.

Down the hatch	Refers to a friendly drink.
Fall foul of	Coming against something wrong.
Freeze the balls off a brass monkey	Cannon balls supposedly would freeze in their brass holder.
Go with the flow	Go with the tide. Or general opinion.
Hand over fist	Pulling up rope quicker using alternate hands.
High and dry	A beached ship.
In the Doldrums	Low spirits. Like a ship in excessively calm water.
In the offing	Predicted. Ship within sight of someone on shore.
Learning the ropes	A beginner.
No room to swing a cat	No room in which to use cat of nine tails.
Pipe down	Stop talking.
Scabby crew	Often used by my brother Derek under duress.
Splice the mainbrace	Celebratory drink.
Spoil the ship for a hap'orth of tar.	Self explanatory.

Sweet Fanny Adams	Pieces of a small girl Fanny Adams found in river 1867.
Swing the lead	Derives from 'swing the leg' or pretending to be ill.
Tell it to the Marines	Sailors were jealous of the Marines saying they would believe anything.
3 sheets in the wind	Out of control. Drunk.
Turn a blind eye	Originating from Nelson's death in 1805.

Some Useful Terms

Although you can get by without knowing any of the correct terms for the parts of a boat, you can be a more helpful crew member if you know a few.

Batten	To cover up and secure hatches.
Battens	Slats of wood put in a sail to retain its shape.
Beam	The widest part of a boat.
Berth	The space allocated to your boat in a marina.
Bilge	The bottom of the boat in the hull to collect bilge water.
Bow	The forward part of a boat.

Cam cleat	A cleat used for quick release by an upward pull.
Capstan	Vertical drum for hoisting the anchor.
Cast off	To let go the mooring lines.
Close haul	Sailing a boat about 45 degrees off the wind.
Draught	The depth of the boat below the waterline.
Fish hooks	Small broken strands on the rigging
Gooseneck	When the sails swing either side of the boom.
Gunwale	The boat's rail.
Heads	The ship's toilet.
Luff	The leading edge of a sail.
Painter	A rope on the bow of a small boat.
Pulpit	A safety rail encircling the bow.
Reach	Various meanings but also the distance between 2 bends in a river.
Reef	Reducing the area of a sail by rolling it up on the boom.
Rowlocks	Swivelling metal rests for boat's oars.

Sheets	Ropes attached to the boom or sail to control it.
Shrouds	Ropes or wires to support mast on either side.
Spar	Wooden or metal boom to give shape to sails.
Spinnaker	A lightweight sail set in the front of a boat.
Stanchion	A strong upright supporting lifelines.
Stays	Ropes or wires supporting the mast.
Tack	To alter course through the eye of the wind.
Tell tale	Strings tied to sails to show wind direction.
Tiller	Lever connected to rudder for steering.
Warp	Heavy line for various purposes.

Ship's Radio

It may be regarded as a luxury to have a ship's radio on a small sailing boat like *Aeolus* but I have always thought of it as a necessity. Sometimes dangerous situations may arise which were not anticipated. I feel so much more at ease knowing I can call for assistance if we need it.

If you sail in a group, it is so easy to keep in touch, listen out for the coast guard, or call up the marina or port where you are heading to hear whether they can accommodate you for the number of nights you require.

I realise that a mobile phone is often used as a substitute but a ship's radio has a longer range. Sometimes there is no signal for a mobile phone. On *Aeolus* we have both. However, when in a marina, the ship's radio should not be used. This is the time to use the mobile phone to contact friends.

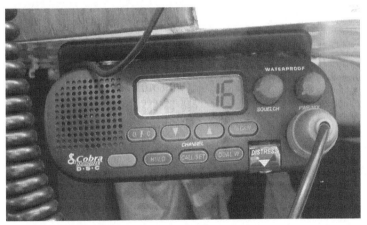

When our original radio went 'kaput' on *Aeolus* after 25 years (they don't make things to last these days) we had to buy a new one. I took the course for a Maritime Radio Operators Certificate of Competence when we first bought *Aeolus*. However because there were more technical updates on the new radio, I decided to take the course again.

Courses tend to be centred around yacht clubs, however they can be also be taken at adult education centres. The courses usually last for one day. When I took my most recent course it cost £30.00 for the course and another £25.00 for the official certificate. There is also a small booklet that can be bought directly from the RYA. Their web site is www.rya.org.uk. In reading the booklet it will reinforce all you will have learnt on the course. Perhaps, and maybe most important of all the book has a photocopiable page which should be kept by the radio in case of an emergency.

There is a set pattern of speech on the radio which although not always observed, is not hard to use, and makes life much simpler if it is adhered to.

For example:

OUT when   conversation is finished.

Not 'over and out' which would indicate you have more to say.

OVER when you want a reply.

SAY AGAIN when you are uncertain of the message.

MAYDAY MAYDAY MAYDAY to be transmitted on **Channel 16** when you are in dire trouble following procedure as set out in the RYA booklet. Many of the distress words derive from the French language. Mayday from M'aidez. Still easy to remember !

PAN-PAN when distress has occurred but not life threatening.

SEELONCE MAYDAY when these words are heard on **Channel 16** , it means silence must be maintained for the sake of another vessel's safety and it must not be broken until the words **SEELONCE FENEE** are heard.

All in all the course is really worth taking for giving such a feeling of achievement when you know you are using the correct procedures.

Radio Check

Thames Coast Guard, Thames Coast Guard
Yacht Tricky, Yacht Tricky

Yacht Tricky, Thames Coast Guard.

Thames Coast Guard, Yacht Tricky,
Can I have a radio check please?

Receiving you loud and clear Sir.

Thank you Thames Coast Guard,
OUT.

Phonetics

Aeolus	Gratitude	Sapper
Alpha	Golf	Sierra
Echo	Romeo	Alpha
Oscar	Alpha	Papa
Lima	Tango	Papa
Uniform	India	Echo
Sierra	Tango	Romeo
	Uniform	
	Delta	
	Echo	

Things to do on a boat

There's lots you have to do on a boat
It's not just a question of keeping afloat
You keep the boat free of slime and weed
Then there's always the ducks to feed.

The route to plan, the forecast to hear
The wine to chill and the drinking of beer
The swans to admire, the cygnets to count
The flag on the rear of the stern to mount.

The lifebelt to check, the ropes to untangle
Keeping out of the sun's such a wrangle.
The hat to put on, sun cream to apply
Keeping an eye on the sea and the sky.

To doze in comfort and try not to gloat
There's such a lot to do on a boat.

The Man who loved Food
(Sailing companion ?)

He loved food,
Not even the glib remark of a salesman
Could spoil his enjoyment of eating.
Orange pieces with chocolate,
Fish and chips, Chinese takeaways
Peaches with white bread
Even when sprayed with dust
From passing cars,
Juicy steaks and new potatoes
He described with zest.

The amazing thing was
To skinny diet watchers
His cholesterol was normal
Blood pressure perfect.

Is there no justice?
Tucking in as art form
All his years would proclaim
Eating for pleasure – and no one to blame.

Birds and Sailing

One hobby which goes nicely with sailing is bird watching. It seems to me that sea birds have to be much more resilient than those on shore. I find the cormorant a most striking bird with its exceptional silhouette as it poises on any protuberance to dry its wings. Then there are the ever present sea gulls. Their persistent cries seem almost unearthly at times. When they go quiet you can bank on an impending storm.

Swans on the river are a regal sight. Coming out of the Port of Ipswich we saw proud parent swans leading the way for their six tiny cygnets, seemingly unaware of the big ships. Unfortunately swans can also be a bit of a pest. At Woodbridge Marina they are almost ferocious, demanding bread by knocking their beaks on the side of the boats and refusing to take no for an answer.

My favourite bird sound is from the tiny skylark who can be heard singing high over the nearby river banks reminding us of the joys of summer. We have also heard the distinctive cry of the peewit in these areas.

Many types of birds can be found on or near rivers, including egrets and storks patiently treading over the shallow waters looking for food in the evening. Unfortunately they are always a bit too far away to take a decent photograph.

Birds commonly found near Essex and Suffolk rivers:

Cormorant

Curlew

Dark bellied Brent Geese

Dunlin

Egret

Gulls many varieties and ever constant

Heron

Little Tern

Peewit

Redshank (easily distinguishable by its red legs)

Reed Bunting

Shelduck

Skylark

We will add to this list as and when we see other bird species. We have a pocket book on birds on *Aeolus* and try to identify as many as we can as we sail along.

Seagulls Haiku

Seagulls crying in the sky

Or are they laughing?

It all depends on your mood.

Cormorant at Tollesbury

The cormorant stands
On old black wreck
And spreads his wings
To dry.

Scarecrow stiff he stands
Before taking off again
And diving down;
I count to seventeen

Before he emerges.
Tiny fish held by gimlet beak
A startled shimmering
Against the sky.

FISH and FISHING

Many species of fish inhabit our East Coast rivers. A good source of information on fish and their habitats can be found by checking out www.suffolkcoastandheaths.org

Our grandchildren used to catch crabs. We would fill the well of *Aeolus* with water to indulge them. However we always let the crabs go afterwards.

There are many rules on the correct sizes of which may be caught and kept. It is very worthwhile to follow the advice of the National Federation of Sea Anglers at www.nfsa.org.uk Information on individual fish can be found on www.fishonline.org

Here is our guide as to what sea life is around and when.

May to February. The Thornback Rays are present inshore. The different species include the smaller spotted, cuckoo or starry rays. Only mature fish may be caught and guidance from the sources mentioned above should be followed at all times.

May to September. There are Bass with a legal minimum landing size of 37cm. Bass can live in excess of 25 years! The females do not mature until they are 5 – 8 years old and measure 40-45cm.

Soles with a legal minimum landing size of 24cm. may be caught from **April to October**. They are right eyed fish, (i.e. both eyes are on the right side of the body). They mature between 3 -5 years old.

May to September is the time for eels. They have an amazing life. In 1904, a Danish biologist, Johannes Schmidt discovered that eels are hatched in the Sargasso Sea, located around the Bermuda Islands and the Azores in the North Atlantic. They then make the perilous journey by migrating across the Atlantic to develop in fresh water rivers. When they are mature at 35-45cm long they return to the Sargasso to breed and then die. Anglers **should not** fish for eels as they are becoming very rare.

June to February. Our favourite fish, the Cod, was in danger of being overfished but it has now been reported that stocks have improved, especially in the Suffolk, Orfordness and Felixstowe areas. There is a legal minimum landing size of 35cm. They reach maturity at 4 – 5 years old.

May to September. Mullet can be seen round jetties and marinas. Although they look easy to catch on account of their slow speed and proximity to the boat, they can be quite difficult as they are very thin lipped and do not fall for the bait easily. Fish under 35cm should not be kept.

June to November. These are the months for the Flounder. They are very similar to plaice except for the bony nodules on their backs. They bury themselves in the sand in daytime but feed at night in shallow water. They can live for up to 15 years. Immature fish under 25cm long may not be kept.

However once again, I must stress guidance from the sources mentioned at the beginning of this chapter should always be adhered to.

Buoys at Sea

When sailing into a river, it is important to know the rule of the buoys. There are two main ones, the **Port** buoy - red - to be kept on the left hand side, and the **Starboard** buoy – green - to be kept on the right.

An easy way to remember this is to say to yourself 'There is no red port left in the bottle'. Not only do these buoys show the way into the river but they may also be there to indicate that on either side of them there may be shallow water where you will get stuck if you are unlucky.

A few times I have let my concentration slip. We have got stuck on a mud bank and had to wait several hours before the water rose sufficiently for *Aeolus* to float off again.

Once we were stuck on a mud bank for the greater part of a day. Furthermore, to our horror *Aeolus* began to tilt over at a steep angle. Paul had to perform some derring-do to get off the boat and tie *Aeolus'* mast to a stake on the bank for safety just in case she tipped over onto her side. It was our wedding anniversary and our daughter, Debbie, was with us. We had arranged to meet my brother Derek for a celebratory meal in Orford. Instead we had quite an enjoyable time playing scrabble, then a game called estimation whist .

A later inspection of *Aeolus'* hull revealed a strong industrial plastic bag had wrapped itself round her prop, so in a way it was highly fortuitous that we had been caught on this bank. We could have sailed on regardless and completely fouled up the engine. Blessings come in strange disguises!

It is interesting to note the origin of the names of the buoys. Years ago in England, the starboard was the steering paddle or rudder. Ships were steered from the right side on the back of the vessel. Larboard was the left side but due to the confusion between the two names it was changed to Port.

Port referred to the opening for cargo on the left of the ship. These terms were officially adopted by the United States Navy in the early 19th century.

Birds and Buoys

The birds use the buoys
As personal perches
They don't seem to mind
How much it lurches.

Back and forth
To and fro
You've got to admire
Their get up and go

Other Buoys and Markers

Markers at sea are very important because they warn of danger such as sand banks, old wrecks and other obstacles. A small illustrated chart can be stuck on the side of the cabin as a reminder if you find it difficult to remember what it is different buoys are trying to point out.

There are the **Cardinal Buoys**. These are based on points of a compass. It is essential you sail in the direction they indicate. The **Keep West** buoy is yellow and black with two black arrows on top pointing towards each other resembling a wine glass which means:

SAIL ON THE WEST SIDE BECAUSE THERE IS A DANGER ON THE EAST SIDE.

The **Keep North** buoy has two black arrows at the top pointing upwards. The **Keep South** buoy has two black arrows at the top pointing down. The **Keep East** buoy has two black arrows with points one up and one down with their bases touching. It is best, I find, to refer to the chart just to confirm you are right. A long black and red striped buoy also warns of a danger. It is known as *Dennis the Menace*. So Watch Out!!

Birds love perching on all these buoys. Their silhouettes look remarkable from a distance on the taller ones. They really look like sentinels.

In fact birds often don't care where they perch. They find a home on some boats even where their owners have taken great trouble to erect strings of shiny used CD discs to try and deter these lively souls from perching there.

Anchoring

If you drop anchor in the daytime, it is best to warn oncoming boats that you are not moving by hoisting a black ball high into the rigging. At night a lantern similarly placed will also act as a warning.

Even despite these precautions, you can find yourself in greater danger moored with an anchor chain rather than on a mooring.

The sea bed may be too loose to take an anchorage, or there may be old wreckage that can entangle the anchor.

Sometimes the anchorage chain may prove too long and you could find yourself far too close for comfort to another boat. Paul has occasionally had to dash on deck in his pyjamas to investigate a strange noise or clanking. It is best to examine the chart to find out the anchorage places then bear fully in mind the proximity of the other boats.

Tides

No book about sailing would be complete without a mention of the tides. *Aeolus* is on a deep sea mooring at Stone, but the tides always have to be considered, together with the weather and wind direction, especially as we are 'fair-weather sailors'.

Sometimes eager young parents have asked us if we could take them and their children out for a day's sailing, however we nearly always have to refuse. This is because an imminent change of weather for the worst has been forecast and no chances can be taken, especially with youngsters.

Once I stood by the mast watching the flow of the tide after having been told we would leave on the 4pm tide. As 4pm approached I saw the moment the tide, after heading slowly in one direction, appeared to stop before swirling around and moving in the opposite direction. What an amazing force it is!

However, there is nothing like harnessing the wind and the tide together. With the sails billowing forth and the tide flowing in the direction you want to go, it is truly remarkable how much progress you can make. Perhaps that is a lesson for life as well. Go with the flow! Happy sailing!

The Royal National Lifeboat Institution

Ordinary amateur yachtsmen have so much to be thankful for with the RNLI. It is a charity, run by fund raising and manned mainly by brave volunteers.

It was founded in 1824 by Sir William Hillary who lived on the Isle of Man and was inspired to start this service by the sight of the many shipwrecks the occurred there. Since then over 139,000 lives have been saved.

Grace Darling, who with her father saved lives from the SS Forfarshire in 1836, is an example of one of these courageous people who risked their lives to save others in difficulty.

There are some magnificent modern lifeboats to be looked at round the coast, but a visit to the Lifeboat Museum at Walton-on-the-Naze reveals the *James Stevens No 14,* built in 1900 and one of the world's oldest surviving motor lifeboats. It has now been restored by volunteers, some of whom were descendants of her original crew. With the aid of funds from the Heritage Lottery, English Heritage Trust, Esme Fairbairn Foundation, local fund raising and sponsorship, they have achieved the seemingly impossible task of restoring her to full seamanship.

In 1894 James Stevens, a Birmingham businessman, left £50,000 to R.N.L.I to build 20 lifeboats. The *James Stevens No 14* was built at the Thames Ironworks in Bow Creek. During her working life she was launched 126 times and saved 227 lives.

When I first saw *James Stevens* she was tied to a jetty at Titchmarsh Marina. She was officially re-launched in 2009 by the television personality Griff Rhys Jones in front of 2,000 people who had come to applaud the enormous effort involved in her restoration.

The End of the Season

The last sail of the season is always a bit sad. Some owners will be relinquishing their boats and selling them on and others know they should be giving up, but hang on for the possibility of another season.

Others, like Paul and myself, will see their boats settled on a hard stand by the yacht club. This enables them to return whenever possible throughout the winter and spring, to give their boats the best maintenance they can, before scurrying back to their warm centrally heated homes.

A date is usually fixed in late spring for re-launching the boats. Obviously there is much to be checked if you are a conscientious owner.

Some boats are left in the sea all winter if their insurance allows for it. Others are given a cursory check on the hard.

Aeolus is a well maintained little craft and although quite old she often draws admiring comments and glances. Two years ago, when her original paintwork was deteriorating Paul set to work. He rubbed down the hull, filled in any dibs and dobs, then put on primer, undercoat and topcoat in her colours of dark royal blue. This was done with such care that it is often mistaken for the original finish.

The old anti fouling had to be taken back to the gel coat and filled in as required. Then, as there was no osmosis, a special white fiberglass primer was applied. After this a silver undercoat was put on followed by the usual antifouling.

New sails were ordered. New windbreakers were purchased with *Aeolus'* name proudly presented on the side. General maintenance on the inside included a new toilet being installed. The choice of course is up to the owner but all these details should be attended to before you set sail again.

At the end of the season, the mooring chain needs to be inspected. The buoy and the thick interwoven line attached to the top part of the mooring chain called the multi plat are pulled in. Both chain and multi plat are then carefully looked at. If all is in order they are replaced by a rope and winter keeper buoy. If they do not look satisfactory to survive the next season, the whole sinker and chain should need to be removed to the beach by a tug -and the chain is replaced.

There is much hard work to keep a sailing boat in good condition but as she takes to the water next season "ship shape and Bristol fashion", it will all have been worthwhile.

Aeolus in Winter

Aeolus is out of the water
Stood high and dry on her keels
Awaiting a rubbing and scrubbing
And a checking of all of her seals.

She waits like a silent warrior
Away from the battle's pain
Through winter's ice and snow
And persistent pattern of rain.

Then the first warm rays awake her
And about her's a kind of glow
She knows that the time awaits her
When once more the action is go.

She slides into the sea
By the frolicsome waves she is chased
She opens her sails with pleasure
As by sea and sky she's embraced.

On Stone Beach

As I stand alone at the edge of the sea
Holding my dinghy close to me
I feel the pull of the rope on my hands
And see the churn and the grind of the sands.

Aeolus dances – a spirit free
On the horizon away from me
And in those moments twixt wait and sail
I feel an enveloping force prevail.

And part of the elements
Part of the scene
No longer alone
But a being supreme.

At one with the earth the sky and the sea
Forever amazed it is all part of me.

Aeolus' Log – 15th Jun - 13th July
and general observations

Wednesday 15th June

Bright day. Wind favourable. South Westerly.
Set off from Stone 11a.m. Sailed to Pyefleet. Realised
we had forgotten our lucky mascot Teddy !
Had nice sail round without resorting to using the
engine. Picked up a mooring. A couple came over in

a boat to tell us
they had lived on
their boat for a
whole year, and
were in charge of
collecting mooring
fees of £10.00
per night for
the owner of the
oyster sheds As there are no facilities at Pyefleet,
I felt it was exorbitant. Paul however negotiated
a deal, saying we expected 2 more boats so could we
have a discount. A small discount was agreed.
Gratitude and Sapper arrived 7.20pm.
Found my Radio competence certificate. Result! I
had looked everywhere for it.
AEOLUS MMSI Call sign MEJQ8 Licence no 1-8444-
55733

DeK's MSI 235084975

Thursday 16th June

Weather forecast: Wind SW backing 5 to 7. Lightening and thunder a.m.

Awoke after a fairly cold night, despite hot water bottle! Derek and Brian came for coffee. Paid mooring fees to the guardian of the creek. Saw a man in a large unusual type boat cleaning oysters ready for sheds. Told they were eaten raw and alive !! Cleaned with pure water as risk of botulism.

Sailed on genoa only round to River Orwell. Arrived as tide turned going out. Picked up mooring opposite Suffolk Y.C. **HAILSTONES!**

Thursday 16th June cont.

Settled for the evening but a call came from Derek thinking that Paul had fallen overboard. BUT: A Seal was trying to climb into the dinghy. Could not believe it! The dinghy nearly overturned. Grabbed camera but too late! 3 hours later to our disbelief, the Seal tried again. Paul dashed onto the deck and shone a powerful torch at him. We saw his amazed seal face giving us a strange look before he dropped off and swam away. We went uneasily to bed wondering if we had seen the last of him because if he turned the dinghy upside down it would have been a problem to right it again.

Friday 17th June

Weather Southerly, force 5 to 7, turning SW 7 to 9. Rain then showers. Brian told us that the seal had also tried to board his dinghy. It was half full of water. 9.am Andrew Summers, from Essex Hundred came, to take photos of us sailing towards Pin Mill. He then came on board and we motored further along to Pin Mill where we dropped him off.

We rowed ashore at Pin Mill and walked up the hill to buy some provisions. Spoke to a customer in the shop about the seal incident and she told us it was a fairly common event in that part of the river. How strange!

Came back to previous mooring with Derek and Brian. . Plans to sail tomorrow to Ipswich at 8.30 am.

Evening 17th June Cont: Awful night with very strong winds and rough sea. Surprisingly slept well but worried that the boat would break away from the mooring.

Saturday 18th June

Woke early. Got going at 8.30 a.m. Arrived at Port Ipswich after motoring all the way up the river. Contacted Port on Channel 68 to notify them of our arrival.

Then booked in to Haven Marina using channel 80. Allocated Row K number 9.

Paul and I went shopping at Ipswich. I bought a new small rucksack and a pair of leather walking shoes from charity shop.

Sunday 19th June

Gave Father's day card to Paul from Debbie. Boiled egg for breakfast. Had shower and hair wash but shock – water was cold! Spoke to a very adventurous lady who had sailed from France in 'Cerebos'.

Tidied up boat. Paul put washing in the washing machine and got it dried .Had lovely salad for lunch enjoying peace after hectic time. Had a rest.

Walked to Christchurch Mansion using map. Open each day not Mondays. Same as museums. Tel 01473 433554 Met some nice guides at the Mansion. So helpful and knew their history. Shelley was exceptional.

I was very interested in a story about Mary Catchpole, 1762 – 1819, a Suffolk country girl employed by the brewing family the Cobbolds, who fell in love with a smuggler. She was transported to Australia in 1800 for horse theft and after a life of adventure eventually died there on the 13th May 1819. There is a book about her which I cannot wait to read and a portrait of her at Christchurch. There is also a very striking black chalk drawing of a boat being towed along at a strange angle, called 'The ghost of Margaret Catchpole. Oooer it did appeal to my sense of the creepy !!

Evening of Sunday 19th June

Met a Dutchman, Goos or Goss (pronounced Ghost with no 'T') on Doffer (meaning 'pincushion'). This was quite an old wooden boat started in 1943 and completed in 1944. All had drinks on Sapper. He pointed out that our sea charts were very antiquated.

Heard that another friend Ashley, on 'Pendragon' was in trouble at Pinmill. His mooring had become snagged. Luckily two members of Benfleet Yacht club were on hand to give assistance.

Monday 20th June still at Ipswich.

Had a shower. Nice and hot this time. Aeolus joined by very large boat to port named Elegance 70 a huge motor cruiser. The carpet men arrived to fit her with a new carpet. How the other half live!!

Ashley arrived in Pendragon, none the worse for wear.

Had lunch then went shopping with Paul. Bought new deck shoes in Simpson's sale, and 'The Death Instinct' by Jed Rubenfeld from a charity shop. Little lady behind counter gave me a look when I picked it out as if to say that's a morbid choice. But I had so enjoyed 'The Interpretation of Murder' by the same author, I decided to give it a whirl. Derek showing signs of a chesty cough. Luckily he has some antibiotics on board.

Tuesday 21st June

Visited Ipswich Museum. What a fantastic museum. Just a delight to see and such very helpful staff.

I was intrigued by a display of Eskimo exhibits. Kayaks and a water proof suit made in 1850 out of seal intestines.

I was moved to copy a poem on display, called 'An Old Man's Song' translated by Rasmussen,

An Old Man's Song

I call to mind
And think of the early coming of Spring
As I knew it In my younger days.
Was I ever such a Hunter?
Was it myself indeed? For I see
And recall in memory,
A man in a Kayak.
Slowly he toils along in towards the shores of the lake.
With many spear-slain caribou in tow.
Happiest am I In my memories of hunting in Kayak.
And an old man, seeking strength in his youth.
Loves most to think of the deeds, Whereby he gained renown.

Information on the Eskimos told us that they learnt to use the kayak at the age of 8 to 10 years old. No wonder they are so skilful.

Having staggered away in awe at all these sights, there were more delights to come. Not least the Egyptian exhibition with exhibits brought to England in 1850. It houses the coffin of Lady Tahathor from Thebes who lived 2,500 years ago, together with a tape telling you about her lifestyle in a most realistic way. The exhibition has been put together with imagination and care. Well worth our visit.

To commemorate our wedding anniversary tomorrow, Paul bought me a small ammonite stone in beautiful shades of green and brown from the Museum Shop. (£1.50 last of the big spenders !)

We later went for a Shepherd's pie in a small café run by Indians but with their idea of English food. Hence a hint of curry in the mashed potato.

Tuesday 21st June evening.
Ashley's boat was boarded by revellers in the night and he had to call Port Security. He was refunded the price of one night's staying in the Marina.

Wednesday June 22nd.
Derek met us on board with a cup of tea to celebrate our wedding anniversary. Paul, Derek and I set off to see Christchurch Mansion again. Such an intriguing place with a fascinating history. It is open Tuesday to Sunday with varied opening times depending on the time of year. Best to telephone before you visit especially if you are hoping for a guided tour. Tel 01473 433554.
Our tour guide was a charming lady, Vicki, who had been conducting this tour since 1996.

154

She certainly knew her subject and pointed out so many subtle details which you would have missed if you had undertaken the tour on your own.

Such as the veiled truth sculpture over one of the fireplaces, the leather jack or jug, and an explanation behind Gainsborough's portrait of the head of Tom Peartree in the Gallery. We had a pot of tea in the tearooms and bought a tiny furry toy hedgehog, for £1.50, Mr Tiggywinkle, as a substitute for our mascot Teddy until he can rejoin us again. We hope they will get on when they eventually meet up!

We then went back to the boat for our lunch of soup and bread and watched as it started to pour with rain.

In the afternoon, we all went for a walk in the grounds of Christchurch manor. This time Brian came with us and we marvelled at the beauty and extent of the grounds. We could easily imagine how it was appreciated in times gone by when ordinary folk were allowed to enjoy the freedom of the grounds. Came home and had salad for dinner then sat on Brian's boat, Sapper, for 'yarning' until around 9.30p.m.

Could not sleep as it was so cold! All hoping weather would perk up soon.

Thursday 23rd June

Overcast, bad forecast. Had shower. Spoke to Barbara on 'Enchantress' - a motor boat. Derek would like to leave. Paul undecided. Poured with rain again. Paul took washing for laundry then he went shopping while I collected washing. Lovely clean and dry.

155

Had chicken pieces and vegetables for lunch. 4.30 p.m. came back through Port of Ipswich and sailed on jib only under Orwell bridge.

Came past Pin Mill where it was almost impossible to pick up mooring as waves turbulent and we lost our pole. Eventually using spare pole we picked up a mooring with a rope attached. Had soup and new bread for supper.

Friday 24th June

Fair night but buoy bumping against boat woke us up. Paul went out on deck to place a fender against buoy to soften sound.

Debating whether to go to River Butley or Deben. Brian not too well. Could be fumes from his new fridge. Barges arriving for race on Saturday. Paul took some lovely photos of them. Decided to go to River Deben. Despite poor weather had a fair crossing into entrance. Good sail on Gib only. Arrived at Ramsholt Arms at 2.30p.m.

Saw George the Harbour Master. Told him I had written a poem about him. He was not impressed. Said he never read poetry!!

Had salad for evening meal. Decided to go to Maybush pub tomorrow at 11.30.

Saturday 25th June

Not bad night. Cold a.m. but getting warmer. Postphoned going to Maybush for evening meal. Stayed at Ramsholt.

Read 'The Pirates Daughter' by Margaret Cezair Thompson re supposed life of Errol Flynn and his illegitimate daughter. Seems appropriate for reading on board.

156

Sunday 26th June

Picked up Ashley from Pendragon and then all had midday lunch at the Ramsholt Arms.
Roast beef and all the trimmings. It was delicious.
Paul fixed new pump to tap.
Planning to sail to Woodbridge 8.15 a.m. tomorrow.

Monday 27th June

Left Ramsholt at 8.15 a.m Weather fair. Wind favourable. Arrived Woodbridge Marina at 9.30a.m..
Berth no 105 North Arm.
Shopped for bread. Phoned friends Barbara and Alan who were coming for a visit. As it was 'Summer' bought a frozen yoghurt and blackcurrant cone from ice cream parlour.
Bought dressed crab for lunch. Visited super charity book shop . Bought 'Flaubert's Parrot' by Julian Barnes for which I had been searching ages, so was well pleased.
Lovely hair wash and shower. Went on Ashley's boat for a quiz and music evening with some kazoos(?) provided by Derek.

Tuesday 28th June

Very Hot ! Met Hilary and Derek with their boat, a beautiful American yacht, called 'Easter'.
Exchanged poetic ideas and books.
Went shopping. Had lovely tuna salad for lunch.
Rain thunder and lightening !
Went shopping again. Picked up a boat hook from Andy Seedhouse 'Aladdin's Cave. Got some grips for boat hook from bike shop. Bought some lovely strawberries from the Co-op for tomorrow, for our visitors.

Poured thunder and lightening again. Got fairly soaked. Power cut in main block of marina. Hilary came and wanted to buy my poetry book. I promised to contact her when I got home.

Wednesday 29th June

Tomorrow leaving Woodbridge for Ramsholt or Pretty Man's Point. Did washing in washing machine. Phoned Barbara to see what time she would be arriving and booked dinner tonight for all of us at the Anchor Pub for 6.30.

Met a remarkable lady in the shower who sailed her 21 foot Jaguar on her own!

Barbara and Alan arrived and we had lovely lunch with ham and Suffolk bread followed by strawberries and yoghurt on board Aeolus. They brought back our mascot Teddy. We are so pleased. Seems to get on well with Mr Tiggywinkle whom we now call Hedgy!

Went for walk along sea wall after Alan bought 2 belts from the sheepskin shop. We previously did our annual shop there and bought gloves and sheepskin slippers. It is such a unique shop. We look forward to visiting it every year.

www.leatherandsheepskinltd.co.uk

Had our meal at the Anchor pub. Treated Derek for his birthday. Plus gave him a copy of Southend Poetry Anthology. Saw Barbara and Alan to their room at the Station guest house.

Thursday 30th June

Still at Woodbridge. Had showers got going early. Shopping. Left Woodbridge 12 noon. Sailed to near Ramsholt to pick up a mooring.. Paul tried out new 'hook'. It was very good. Listened to News – teachers' strike.

158

Friday 1st July

Weather fair, wind slight.

As leaving Ramsholt saw 1 of 600 little ships that went to Dunkirk.

'Maid Marion' PZ 61. A 39.5 ft blue Cornish lugger on her Summer berth at Ramsholt, now owned by David Hunt of Braintree.

She was nearly wrecked 3 years ago when a modern ship rammed into her. Harbour master George Collins saved her from sinking.

Approaching Felixstowe Ferry Aeolus got stuck on mud. Luckily tide was rising.

Crossed over from Deben. Sailed to Walton Backwaters. Picked up a mooring. Booked into Titchmarsh Marina for tomorrow 9.30- 10 am.

G31 for Derek G27 for us G33 for Brian.

Felt worried that little grandson Oscar's birthday card would not reach him by 4th July. Flagged down a team of lady rowers who offered to take the card and post it for me.

Saturday 2nd July

Moored in Walton Backwaters.

Got up at 7.20 a.m.. Wished Derek 'Happy Birthday'.

9.30 a.m. gently sailed to Titchmarsh Marina. Found berth and managed to tie up on our own. Booked in at Harbour Lights restaurant for 6 pm. Had shower and washed clothes. Had lunch as our visitors Barbara and Alan would be late.

When they arrived took them to their nice little Edwardian guest house overlooking the sea. No parking but some available in car park behind house. Did shopping then drove back to Marina.

159

Had lovely carvery for £5.95. Went to look at Halda on our yearly pilgrimage to this lovely little boat gently rotting away. Then visitors went back to their guest house. Derek and Brian rounded off evening by coming for mugs of hot chocolate.

Sunday 3rd July

Lazy morning, then walked to Frinton. Charity shops were open so had browse. Bought 'Brown Owl's Guide to Life' by Kate Harrison. Shopped in Co op walked home. After dinner walked to see the old life boat the Robert Stevenson. Took photo. Also an unusual boat on the Marina, slightly Chinese looking called 'Skylark'.

7 pm had sherry and yarns with Brian and Derek. Tomorrow they must go home to a take delivery of a new suite of furniture and other business. They will go by taxi to station then take a bus home and return by car.

Monday 4th July

Oscar's birthday. Age 3. He got his card so the ladies saved the day. Derek and Brian left for home. We miss them already. Paul and I took sandwiches and walked to Walton. Went to RNLI shop. Bought notepad and Christmas Cards! Had dinner then went to talk to Graham, a retired London taxi driver, who was working to restore a Snapdragon, 'Emerald Girl'. He had made so many modifications but in view of his failing eyesight it seemed unlikely he would ever sail in her.

Phoned Oscar, age 3, for his birthday and spoke to sister Sophia age 7. She is taking sailing lessons. 'Permission to come aboard!' is what she tells me you must say when you board a boat. Brian gave me a strange look when I tried it out while boarding 'Sapper' a few days later!

160

Tuesday July 5th

Leisurely morning. Winds severe but as tucked up in Marina this did not bother us. It was strange to see the usually calm waters really tossing about though.

Salad lunch, then walked to Frinton. Lovely partially undercover shopping centre called 'The Triangle'. Looked at charity shops again and at the Co-op supermarket bought 'A Taste of Essex' recipe book.

Wednesday July 6th

Storm and tempest. Very windy. Had shower and cleared up Aeolus. Read book. Derek and Brian returned. Gave Brian a small gift of a mug with a Betty Boop motif on it and Derek some brown flannels he needed as his had blown overboard.

Put washing in machine. Had smoked fish for dinner. Took photos of Halda. Again feel an enduring sadness at the demise of this valiant little boat.

Thursday July 7th

Had Paul's very thick porridge for breakfast. Still too windy to leave Marina.

As Derek and Brian had returned to Marina in Derek's car, we decided to all go to Clacton. Very Blowy. Plenty of charity shops. Decided to have a treat in Wetherspoons and all had steak and kidney puddings in rich gravy. Yum!

Got back to Aeolus. Looked at weather forecast on Chandlery wall.

Winds continuing. Gales tomorrow. Hot water bottles in sleeping bags!

Friday July 8th

Heavy rain in night. Went with Derek and Brian to Frinton in Derek's car. A real treat but would prefer to be sailing on Aeolus. Did some more shopping and washing. Found Tesco washing tablets to be very good. Got a French book from laundry room where you can take a book or pop one in for others, 'Cromwell' by Victor Hugo. A play in French, should keep the brain cells active while enduring this wild 'Summer' weather.

Saturday July 9th

Still rough but decided to go as winds slightly better than yesterday. North Westerly, force 5 to 7.
Had shower and change of clothes. Set off at 9.45 a.m. Very windy. Sailed 7 hours on rough sea. Just had a rough ham sandwich and a biscuit. on the way. So rough, could not even visit the heads!
5 pm .Arrived at Pyefleet Creek. Paul dropped an anchor. 45 feet of anchor chain to 6 metres of depth. Had evening meal of lamb chops and spinach. So rough Brian lost hearing aid overboard.
Radio seems to be playing up.

Sunday July 10th

Weather much improved, wind South Easterly, force 5 to 7.
Favourable for Gratitude and Sapper to sail to Leigh. Sad to see them go at 11.30 a.m. but decided to stay at anchor for a while longer and enjoy Pyefleet.
Took sandwiches and rowed ashore. Very nice walk along new public footpath we found to the Country Park. Tide on turn to come home so easy row for Paul. Got very muddy getting into dinghy. Lovely meal of minced beef and vegetables on our return. Very tired after sail yesterday. Played Estimation Whist, then early to bed .

Monday July 11th

Lifted anchor and sailed to Brightlingsea. Radio playing up. Eventually managed to contact Harbour Master Brightlingsea to inform him of our intended stay.

Had lunch then rowed ashore. Borrowed child's life jacket from Harbour Master for little great grandson's visit tomorrow.

Had phone call from Derek at Walton as he had to return to pick up his car. He and Brian were having nice meal again at 'Harbour Lights'.

Played cards then bed.

Tuesday July 12th

Good nights rest. 12 Belgian boats came and double moored behind us. Enjoyed practising French with them.

Caught launch to town and met grand daughter Zoe with little Renell age nearly 4.

Did some exciting crabbing with bacon pieces. Renell put on life jacket and we went by launch to Aeolus. We all had bacon sandwiches and cake. Little Renell got a bit bored after a while so Paul rowed him ashore with Zoe while I arrived by launch with the Belgians.

After more crabbing and a visit to the children's play park we all had fish and chips. They then went home and we returned to Aeolus.

Wednesday July 13th

Very strong force 5 to 7 high N – NW winds again. Got up at 6 a.m.

Set sail 8.30a.m.

Sailed very quickly even with both sails reefed round to Bradwell.

Extremely rough seas. Aeolus performed very well.
She seemed to be proving she really was the 'Ruler of
the Winds'

Andrew Summers was at Bradwell to take our photos.
Arrived at Stone. Paul had a difficult row ashore due
to wind and rain. Oh dear – our cruise was over.

Shirley Baker is a poet who finds inspiration where many of us see only the mundane. Currently Secretary of the Southend Poetry Group she is published in many of its anthologies and has read her poetry on television and radio. She has an Open University honours degree in 'Art History and Modern Literature' and has written articles and poetry for various magazines and organizations such as the 'Endeavour Trust' and the 'Dunmow Flitch'. She has also written a medieval play to accompany madrigals for her daughter's secondary school in Zimbabwe.

The first five years of married life with husband Paul, who was in the RAF, was spent in a caravan on a farm in Huntingdon. Since then she has lived in many parts of Britain and Malta and is widely travelled.

She now lives, with Paul, in Leigh-on-Sea, where she went to school at Westcliff High School for Girls. Together they are able to indulge their passion for sailing round the East Coast Rivers in their ancient boat *Aeolus* which they have owned for 26 years.

"This book is a joyous record of some of those journeys and the poetry they inspired."